The
Quadruple
Object

The
Quadruple
Object

Graham Harman

Winchester, UK
Washington, USA

First published by Zero Books, 2011
Zero Books is an imprint of John Hunt Publishing Ltd., Laurel House, Station Approach,
Alresford, Hants, SO24 9JH, UK
office1@o-books.net
www.o-books.com

For distributor details and how to order please visit the 'Ordering' section on our website.

Text copyright: Graham Harman 2010

ISBN: 978 1 84694 700 1

A CIP catalogue record for this book is available from the British Library.

Design: Stuart Davies

Printed in the UK by CPI Antony Rowe
Printed in the USA by Offset Paperback Mfrs, Inc

CONTENTS

The composition of this book was enabled by a Faculty Research Grant from the American University in Cairo, authorized by the good wishes of Provost Lisa Anderson and Vice Provost Ali Hadi, to whom I offer my gratitude.

Further thanks are due to Professor Michael Flower of Portland State University, who expertly prepared the ten helpful diagrams.

Author's Preface to the English Edition

This book first appeared in French as *L'Objet quadruple: Une
métaphysique des choses après Heidegger* (Paris: PUF, 2010), in a
fine translation by Olivier Dubouclez of Lille. The history of the
project shaped the very structure of the book, and may be of
interest to the reader.

For several years Quentin Meillassoux had expressed the
wish to see some of my work appear in French. His initial hope
was to encourage someone to translate my first book, *Tool-Being:
Heidegger and the Metaphysics of Objects* (Chicago: Open Court,
2002). But to publishers in Paris this could only sound like a
costly commitment to an author not yet well known in France.
Even after Meillassoux himself became co-editor of the
MétaphysiqueS series at PUF, the situation looked discouraging.
For a time the project seemed out of reach.

One day, the idea occurred to me of working in reverse.
Rather than tracking down the funds to translate a pre-existing
book, I could first find a grant and then write a new book to fit
it: much like an architect bound to a specific budget and plot of
land. The idea immediately excited me, given my view that
ideas are strongest when shaped by the pressures of local
circumstance. Not surprisingly, Meillassoux himself also saw
merit in the proposal. Immediately I applied for a research grant
at my home institution, the American University in Cairo. The
time has not come to tell the bureaucratic adventure story of the
grant process itself. Suffice it to say that the intervention of two
enlightened administrators saved this book from a premature
death (I have thanked them elsewhere in this book). The check
was cashed in Cairo and calculations were made in Paris. Soon I
was informed by Meillassoux of how long the work should be,
in accordance with PUF's standard translator salary rates.
Though French publishers work according to *signes* rather than

words, the requested length amounted to approximately 47,000 words: a nice, brisk little book. Luckily our translator was already enlisted, and Meillassoux proved correct in his assurances of Dubouclez's skill as a philosopher, a speaker of English, and a French stylist.

But the timing was difficult. For the summer of 2009 I was already committed to a lecture in Croatia, and two lectures and a wedding in England. Thus I was left with only six weeks to write the entire book. Making a virtue of necessity, I decided to "live-blog" the writing of the book for my existing internet readership (see http://doctorzamalek2.wordpress.com). The presence of an audience would supply useful pressure to work hard on the book each day, with the added advantage of being able to give my graduate student readers an inside look at how books are written. From late July through the end of August I posted daily updates on my progress. For curiosity's sake, I also *timed* the writing of the book, and in this way discovered that the final draft of *The Quadruple Object* took 86 hours and 34 minutes to complete.

In addition to constraints on the length of the book, some of its content was shaped by the nature of the audience. The French public was then almost entirely unfamiliar with my work. This meant that I needed to recapitulate the main ideas of my earlier books in such a way as to bring French readers up to speed. But there could not be *too much* recapitulation, or else none of my Anglophone readers would be interested in the inevitable English edition that now lies before you. In this way the unusual content of this book was born: a highly compressed version of my established ideas in the earlier chapters, with forays into new terrain towards the end of the book. I also tried to write more concisely and directly than usual, mimicking one of the best-known strengths of elegant classical French prose. Ultimately I also deleted a few of the more bizarre jokes and images from the French version, after finding that they did not come across especially well in that language. Naturally, I have retained those passages in the English version: keep an eye out for the bigamist South Pacific cult leader. Otherwise, I made changes to the manuscript in *both* languages according to the excellent advice of both Meillassoux and Dubouclez. An extra five thousand words were added at their recommendation, and Dubouclez had the remarkable kindness to translate this additional material free of charge. Finally, my friend Michael Flower (whom I have never met except via email) engineered the attractive diagrams found in the book. Adding these three people to the two administrators in Cairo who saved the grant, that makes at least five people other than myself who made crucial contributions to the very existence of *The Quadruple Object*. If we add the main figures I dealt with at Zer0 Books (especially Tariq Goddard and Mark Fisher) the number grows even larger.

As a philosophy blogger I often provide writing advice to students. One of the things I like to tell them is that the two biggest enemies of writing, the two worst causes of writer's block, are *nothingness* and *infinity*. Nothingness refers to the blank paper or computer screen with which we begin; infinity is the self-imposed pressure to say something of limitless scope and significance. My way of addressing these two closely linked threats is to focus on all the *constraints* on a project that lie beyond my control: the rules I absolutely must follow without having chosen them, and which are obviously neither nothing nor infinite. Simply by identifying all the operative constraints on a given project, one's room for free decision is narrowed and focused to a manageable range, and the specters of nothingness and infinity soon dissipate in the rising sun. When that happens, it becomes possible to summarize your life's work in a mere six weeks of writing. Never have I written something as constrained by budget and audience as the book now in your hands. Nonetheless, it is a perfect distillation both of the familiar thoughts that have occupied me for the past twenty years, and the unfamiliar ones that seem ready to occupy me for the twenty years to come.

Introduction

Instead of beginning with radical doubt, we start from naiveté. What philosophy shares with the lives of scientists, bankers, and animals is that all are concerned with *objects*. The exact meaning of "object" will be developed in what follows, and must include those entities that are neither physical nor even real. Along with diamonds, rope, and neutrons, objects may include armies, monsters, square circles, and leagues of real and fictitious nations. All such objects must be accounted for by ontology, not merely denounced or reduced to despicable nullities. Yet despite repeated claims by both friends and critics of my work, I have never held that all objects are "equally real." For it is false that dragons have autonomous reality in the same manner as a telephone pole. My point is not that all objects are equally real, but that they are equally *objects*. It is only in a wider theory that accounts for the real and unreal alike that pixies, nymphs, and utopias must be treated in the same terms as sailboats and atoms. If this approach reminds some readers of the Austrian theories of objects of the late nineteenth century (Twardowski, Meinong, Husserl) at least two major differences will appear in the course of this book: (1) objects according to my model have a fourfold structure that is drawn from Heidegger; (2) I treat causal relations between non-human objects no differently from human perception of them. But it should also be noted that I do not adopt Heidegger's distinction between "object" (which he uses negatively) and "thing" (which he uses positively). The word "object" acquires in the Brentano School a generalizing power too valuable to be sacrificed to the cult rituals of Heideggerian terminology.

The history of philosophy has already seen numerous theories of individual objects. Beginning with Aristotle's primary substance, these theories lead us through Leibnizian monads, the aforementioned Austrian theories of Husserl and his rivals, and Heidegger's fourfold "thing." Despite my admiration for these worthy ancestors, this book does not aim at a synthesis, but at a new metaphysics able to speak of all objects and the perceptual and causal relations in which they become involved. Rejecting the post-Kantian obsession with a single relational gap between people and objects, I hold that the inter-action between cotton and fire belongs on the same footing as human interaction with both cotton and fire.

Those who deny that objects are the building block of philosophy have only two basic alternatives. They can say that objects are a mere surface effect of some deeper force, so that the object is undermined. Or they can say that objects are a useless superstition in comparison with their more evident qualities or relations, so that the object is "overmined." Let's begin with these two critical strategies and see why they cannot succeed, and why objects must finally prevail. The reader need not fear that the result will be a boring traditional realism of atoms and billiard balls. Instead, objects as presented in this book are as strange as ghosts in a Japanese temple, or signals flashing inscrutably from the moon.

I

Undermining and Overmining

Once we begin from naiveté rather than doubt, objects immediately take center stage. On my desk are pens, eyeglasses, and an expired American passport. Each of these has numerous qualities and can be turned to reveal different surfaces and uses. Furthermore, each object is a unified thing despite its multitude of features. The same is equally true of the non-physical entities that surround me, such as Egypt, Cairo, or the neighborhood of Zamalek. Opening my volume of Gibbon's history of Rome, I find historical objects no longer in our midst, such as Diocletian and the Gnostics. When mathematicians flee from the physical world to their ideal sphere, they still confront objects ranging from integers to cones. The same holds for the centaur, Pegasus, unicorn, and hobbit that absorb my thoughts when work becomes too stressful.

Some of these objects are physical, others not; some are real, others not real in the least. But all are *unified* objects, even if confined to that portion of the world called the mind. Objects are units that both display and conceal a multitude of traits. But whereas the naive standpoint of this book makes no initial claim as to which of these objects is real or unreal, the labor of the intellect is usually taken to be *critical* rather than naive. Instead of accepting this inflated menagerie of entities, critical thinking debunks objects and denies their autonomy. They are dismissed as figments of the mind, or as mere aggregates built of smaller physical pieces. Yet the stance of this book is not critical, but sincere. I will not reduce some objects to the greater glory of others, but will describe instead how objects relate to their own visible and invisible qualities, to each other, and to our own minds — all in a single metaphysics.

7

A. Undermining

The first critical response to objects asserts that they are not fundamental. All of the dogs, candles, and snowflakes we observe are built of something more basic, and this deeper reality is the proper subject matter for philosophy. As the surf pounded the shores of Anatolia, Thales proposed water as the first principle of everything. Later came Anaximenes, for whom air rather than water was the root of the world. It is slightly more complicated with Empedocles, for whom things are composed not of one but of four separate elements: air, earth, fire, and water, joined and divorced through the forces of love and hate. And finally with Democritus, atoms of different shapes and sizes serve as the root element of all larger things. In present-day materialism one speaks instead of quarks or infinitesimal strings. In all such cases, the critical method is the same: what seems at first like an autonomous object is really just a motley aggregate built of smaller pieces. Only what is basic can be real.

One could go much further than this materialism of tiny elements, as several pre-Socratic thinkers did. For there is a certain vulgarity in naming one or more physical elements as lord of the others. Any such theory of basic physical elements appears superficial if we hold instead that reality is fundamentally *one*, and diversity an illusion. Philosophy becomes monism. In ancient Greek thinking this One goes by different names — sometimes *being*, sometimes the boundless *apeiron*. The champions of this notion disagree solely over whether the One existed in the past and was somehow shattered to pieces (Pythagoras, Anaxagoras), exists in the present while our senses deceive us into thinking otherwise (Parmenides), or will exist in the future once justice has done the work of destroying all opposites (Anaximander). Similar examples are found even in recent France: Emmanuel Levinas, with his rumbling *il y a* broken to pieces only by human consciousness;[1] and Jean-Luc Nancy, with his shapeless "whatever" preceding all specific beings.[2] The problem with such theories is that if all is truly one, there seems to be little reason why it should ever break into fragments at all.

It is precisely this worry that often gives rise to a subtler model: a more half-hearted monism of "pre-individual" things. Its origins lie in Anaxagoras, for whom splinters broken from the *apeiron* contain the seeds of everything else: a tree must also contain the encrypted forms of birds, flowers, and fire, making it possible for one thing to transform into another. This theory was resurgent in the wild metaphysics of Giordano Bruno, with his infinite matter laced with enfolded forms that await "contraction" into individual beings.[3] Other such theories were proposed by Gilbert Simondon[4] and now Manuel DeLanda[5] who speaks (in the manner of Bergson) of a "heterogeneous yet continuous" plane of virtuality. Yet if the philosophy of the One has difficulty explaining the emergence of numerous things, and a pluralist philosophy finds it hard to explain their inter-connection, then the appeal to a "pre-individual" realm does not help us much. For if this deeper reality contains seeds of individual things, then these seeds are either distinct from one another or they are not. If not, then we have monism. And if they are distinct, then we have the same situation as in the actual world of objects, with nothing gained but the *assertion* that they are "both connected and unconnected at the same time."

The same problem arises if objects are rejected as too static and dethroned in favor of some "play of difference" or primordial flux of becoming. It might be said that reality itself is flux, and that talk of *objects* merely crystallizes becoming in an abstract state, deprived of its vital inner dynamism. But the same problem arises here as before. For if we say that any specific dog or moon is merely an abstraction from a deeper flux, we still need to ask whether the world is one flux or many. If only one, then we are back with monism. But if many, then each has some sort of specific and integral character, and this already makes it an object. The same holds true for philosophies of difference, which claim that a thing has no identity but instead always differs from itself. For whatever it means to say that an object differs from itself, the fact remains that airplanes, carrots, electrical pylons, triremes, walls, and men differ from themselves in different ways. The philosophy of difference may give us blurry entities laced with negation and relationality, but they are entities nonetheless.

More could be said about each of these strategies. But for our purposes it is enough to call them strategies that *undermine* objects as the root of philosophy. All of them claim that objects are too specific to deserve the name of ultimate reality, and dream up some deeper indeterminate basis from which specific things arise. They find it naive to think of dogs as basic elements of the world, since dogs really must be just aggregates of organic chemicals, or fragments of *apeiron*, or an active "dogging" rather than the stasis of a solid dog-thing, or the result of a long evolutionary struggle with climate and predators. All such strategies assume that a dog, candle, or army is built of some basic physical or historical element whose permutations give rise to these objects as a sort of derivative product. All are versions of reductionism in which objects only gain their reality from elsewhere. All are forms of *critique* that view individual objects in a spirit of nihilism, destroying them with bulldozers to make way for something more fundamental. They view objects as too shallow to be the fundamental reality in the universe.

B. Overmining

A different way of dismissing objects as the chief *dramatis personae* of philosophy is to reduce them upward rather than downward. Instead of saying that objects are too shallow to be real, it is said that they are too deep. On this view the object is a useless hypothesis, a *je ne sais quoi* in the bad sense. Rather than being undermined from beneath, the object is overmined from above. On this view, objects are important only insofar as they are manifested to the mind, or are part of some concrete event that affects other objects as well.

Consider the widespread empiricist view that the supposed objects of experience are nothing but bundles of qualities. The word "apple" is merely a collective nickname for a series of discrete qualities habitually linked together: red, sweet, cold, hard, solid, juicy. What exist are individual impressions, ultimately in the form of tiny pixels of experience, and the customary conjunction of these puncta leads us to weave them into larger units. This empiricist model is seen as so admirably rigorous that even many anti-empiricists adopt it. Nonetheless, it is a pure fiction. For what we encounter in experience are unified objects, not isolated points of quality. Indeed, the relation actually goes in reverse, since the individual qualities of things are already imbued with the style or feel of the thing as a whole. Even if the exact hue of red in my apple can also be found in a nearby shirt or can of spraypaint, the colors will have a different feel in each of these cases, since they are bonded to the thing to which they belong. Husserl made this point vividly in the *Logical Investigations*,[6] but it has not spread widely enough, nor have its consequences been fully drawn.

If empiricism denies that there are objects within human experience, then what about objects *outside* experience? This is a slightly different question. While some recent philosophy has been realist in spirit, the vast majority of avant-garde thinkers since Kant have shown markedly anti-realist traits. For the realist, the existence of objects outside the mind is as real as human experience itself. The anti-realist might counter this attitude with two possible stances. Either the existence of the outside world can be denied outright as in the idealism of Berkeley, with his famous maxim that "to be is to be perceived." Or the world can be treated skeptically, with a tone of agnostic caution. According to this latter standpoint, which Quentin Meillassoux has given the excellent name of "correlationism,"[7] we cannot think of world without humans or humans without world, but only of a primal correlation or rapport between the two. In recent centuries this correlationist stance has seemed like the unavoidable horizon for all cutting-edge philosophy. But at the close of Chapter Four, I will give reasons for why I think it is false.

There is also an intriguing variant of the correlationist position that we might call "relationism." This essentially anti-Kantian theory denies that all reality is grounded in the human-world relation, but still claims that nothing is real unless it has some sort of effect on other things. This position can be found in the philosophies of Whitehead, Latour, and some of the American pragmatists. It holds that the human perception of raindrops falling against a window is no different *in kind* from the relation between the rain and window themselves. All relations are of fundamentally the same variety, in flat contradiction of the correlationist view. Nonetheless, both positions share the notion that a thing's existence consists solely in its relation with other things. An object is exhausted by its presence for another, with no intrinsic reality held cryptically in reserve.

All of these positions overmine the object, treating it as a useless substratum easily replaced by direct manifestations. Though we claim to be speaking of objects, they are really nothing more than palpable qualities, effects on other things, or images in the mind. But there are problems with relationizing the world in this way. For one thing, if the entire world were exhausted by its current givenness, there is no reason why anything would alter. That is to say, if there is no difference between the I who is what he is and the I who is accidentally wearing a yellow shirt from India at this moment, then there is no reason why my situation should ever change. An injustice is thereby done to the future. Another problem is that this position has no way to link different relations together to make them relations to the *same* thing. If a house is encountered by three women, a child, a dog, and a crow in the same moment, each of these perceptions will have a very different character. And given a purely *relational* definition of what objects are, it would seem impossible to call all of them relations to the "same" house. The house itself vanishes into a mob of house-perceptions. Nor would this disaster happen only to houses: for if I take the stage in a crowded auditorium and am witnessed by hundreds of spectators, I would also dissolve into a manifold of *perceptions* of me, each unconnected with the rest. While it is already dubious to link all of the house-perceptions by external "family resemblances," the same maneuver is clearly impossible when we are speaking of the views that spectators have of me. For I am something real, here and now, not a tapestry of perceptions woven together from the outside.

C. Both Extremes at Once

Those who resist the notion that individual objects are the central topic of metaphysics have no other option: the object must either be undermined from below or overmined from above. It is either reduced to some primitive element lying somewhere in the depths, or it is portrayed as a falsely mysterious supplement that can be replaced by what is directly given. Already I have said that monism, the pre-individual, and primordial flux or difference (all of them undermining gestures) are unable to replace the object. And I have also suggested that to an equal degree such overmining notions as idealism, correlationism, relationism, and the empiricist "bundle of qualities" fail to replace the object as well. But we should also briefly discuss a third alternative: materialism. What makes materialism such a special opponent is that it does not merely undermine or overmine the object, but performs both of these maneuvers simultaneously. In this respect, materialism is the hereditary enemy of any object-oriented philosophy.

Consider the early materialisms that arose in ancient Greece. The privileged physical elements of Thales, Anaximenes, and Empedocles all point to a layer deeper than familiar objects such as tables, machines, and horses. Objects are not fundamental for these early Greeks, but are reduced to some physical element that generates them. At first this looks like a textbook example of undermining the object by moving to a deeper level. But consider what is actually obtained once this reduction to physical elements is complete. For in fact there is no concealed mystery in the pre-Socratic notions of water or fire: all such elements have specific, tangible properties that can be exhaustively described and measured. The same holds for more advanced scientific concepts such as atoms. For the atom can be considered as nothing but a hard unyielding particle occupying a distinct point in space-time. And even if that point becomes blurred, as in quantum theory, the sciences still view it in terms of its qualities — namely, its statistical chance of being in certain positions at certain moments. The tiny physical bulk of the atom may be viewed as a substrate for unifying all of its qualities, but this very substrate is taken to be nothing more than a certain set of palpable qualities such as hardness and resistance. In other words, there is no need to regard the atom as an object at all, and the empiricists would instead call it a set of habitually bundled traits, just as they do with the apple.

In this way, materialism both undermines *and* overmines objects by treating them as ultimate elements that are actually nothing but sets of qualities. In this respect, it merely repeats the basic gesture of all philosophies that reject objects as a primal category: for in fact it turns out that every undermining philosophy needs an overmined component as a supplement, and vice versa. Consider the case of a perfect monism claiming that all is one, that the multiplicity of things encountered by the senses is illusory. But these supposed illusions of experience, such as the food and cars and animals that surround me, *are* experienced after all, and must be accounted for by philosophers in some way. For this reason, monism grudgingly accepts our human experience as a kind of unreal supplement of what is solely and truly real — being itself. The same holds for philosophies of the pre-individual. While claiming that actual objects are derivative of some deeper virtual sphere, they do not mean to deny that we experience such objects; they merely hold that these actual entities are secondary. The undermining philosophies cannot deny the more superficial layer of experience that humans undergo: they simply give it a second-rate reality, a supplemental or shadowy existence. But while accounting for the two extremes, they completely skip the intermediate layer of autonomous objects that are both actually individual and also autonomous from all perception.

The same thing often happens in reverse with the overminers of objects. The most famous example is surely Kant, who supplements experience with the ghostly things-in-themselves, which are then largely excluded from further discussion. Even Berkeley and Whitehead must posit God as a special entity able to correlate all our perceptions. There is admittedly a slight asymmetry between this situation and that of the underminers, since some overmining philosophers do abandon every notion of a hidden layer beneath perception, as in the case of German Idealism. By contrast, it is rather difficult to imagine an inverted movement called "German Monism" that would have affirmed the One while denying even an *illusory* existence to sense-experience. After all, such experience is there before us at all times as the very medium in which we live. But many if not all overminers of objects do feel the need to admit some shapeless primal layer of the cosmos beyond direct access. And here we simply have the reverse of the pattern found among the underminers: another leap from one extreme to the other, while autonomous objects are once more excluded as a proper topic of philosophy.

There are exactly two problems with materialism. First, it discounts the possibility of larger emergent entities. Even if all nations of the European Union are composed of quarks and electrons, we can shift these particles around to some extent without changing the Union. There are countless different numbers and arrangements of particles that could be tried without the Union itself being changed. This principle is sometimes known as "redundant causation": numerous different causes can yield the same object, which suggests that the object is something over and above its more primitive elements. Second, just as a real object is irreducible downwards, it is also irreducible *upwards* to its palpable qualities, for reasons that the coming discussion of Husserl and Heidegger should make clear. Physical particles try to undermine and overmine objects at the same time, but fall victim to their own weapons: for objects are both deeper and shallower than material elements can ever be.

D. Objects

Much of the history of philosophy is divided between these two strategies that I have condemned. Yet the insistence of this book that objects should be the hero of philosophy is no lonely or eccentric fiat. To call for an object-oriented theory is simply to pursue an already existing tendency in the history of philosophy, albeit with renewed intensity. For all their magic and charm, the pre-Socratic philosophers reduced objects either to a unified whole or to one or more basic physical elements; in this way, the first Greek philosophers were also opponents of object-oriented philosophy *avant la lettre*. Against Heidegger's claim that pre-Socratic thought guarded the mystery of being while Plato and Aristotle began a long slide into decadent forgetting, I hold that Plato and Aristotle first put philosophy on its true path.

In the Platonic dialogues, we find Socrates in ceaseless pursuit of the definitions of things. It is seldom remembered that

Socrates never *reaches* any such definitions. Such failure is built into the very word philosophy — as *love* of wisdom rather than wisdom itself. This is especially visible in some of my favorite passages in the dialogues. Consider Socrates's admonition to Meno that he should not ask whether virtue can be taught before we know what virtue is. Or recall his similar statement in the *Gorgias* that we cannot ask whether rhetoric is a "fine thing" without first knowing what rhetoric is. Socrates does not make these statements merely to scold the impatience of his inter-locutors, as though they simply needed to wait five or six more pages to obtain accurate definitions of virtue or rhetoric before moving further. The point is deeper than this: unlike gods, we mortals *cannot* know what virtue and rhetoric really are. Nor is it just a matter of limitations on knowledge. Rejecting the pre-Socratic attempt to describe the primal elements of the world in their naked purity, Socrates holds that things are inherently *deeper than their traits*, and in this way he points to a challenging rift between object and quality. And while Platonism has often been condemned for a two-world theory leading to contempt for life and the triumph of vulgar Christianity, the recognition that the object is split in half marks a basic philosophical advance.

Yet for Plato this rift between unknowable virtue and its visible crowd of features plays out not within the object itself, but between the object and a world lying beyond it. Only with Aristotle do individual objects first become the central player in philosophy. For him the important gulf no longer lies between perfect forms and their flawed manifestations in matter. Instead, there are duels underway in the heart of objects themselves: between an individual cat and its fleeting accidental features, or even between that cat and its essential qualities. In every period of philosophy where Aristotle has had influence, specific entities have gained in stature and dignity. This is true for the Scholastic period that proverbially followed Aristotle's star, and is equally true of his magnificent heir Leibniz, whose

Aristotelianism is rudely airbrushed from history by Deleuze.[8] The monads are individual things, but as unified things they differ from the multitude of qualities that they must possess. While it is true that Leibniz defines the monads by their perceptions of other things, what is more important is that these perceptions are not in genuine contact with the other monads, none of which have windows. A monad's relations with its peers are given by God from the dawn of time.

These theories of Aristotle, Leibniz, and their allies can all be called theories of substance. The object-oriented philosophy proposed in this book is the latest theory in the same lineage. Yet the theory proposed here is significantly weirder, since it rejects many of the features traditionally ascribed to substance. Above all, there has been a tendency to hold that substances must be natural. A tree can be a substance, but not a plastic cup; dolphins or stones are substantial, but not a windmill or a circle of men holding hands. In Leibniz there is the further unfortunate tendency to identify the substance with what is *simple*, which forbids him from granting monads to a pair of diamonds glued together or the Dutch East India Company. The Leibnizian distinction between substance and aggregate implies a two-world theory in which a final layer of ultimate monads is opposed by a derivative plane of complicated aggregates that are nothing but "things of reason" rather than realities. And there is another regrettable feature of monads that actually represents a backslide from Aristotle: namely, Leibniz's view that substances must be *indestructible*. With his primary substances, Aristotle was the first philosopher in ancient Greece to propose ultimate realities that can be destroyed. It is not difficult to annihilate a horse, for instance. But for Leibniz this would be impossible, since the horse-monad cannot be destroyed any more than a human monad can. Another feature of traditional substance is that it must be real. Creatures of myth might dance before the mind, but in no way are they substances.

Yet all of these traditional features of substance must be rejected. Objects need not be natural, simple, or indestructible. Instead, objects will be defined only by their autonomous reality. They must be autonomous in two separate directions: emerging as something over and above their pieces, while also partly withholding themselves from relations with other entities. Instead of radical attempts to reduce reality to some more basic root, whether it be particles, the *apeiron*, images in the mind, bundles of qualities, or pragmatic effects, the object turns out to be *polarized* into two irreducible segments. While this book will endorse a classical-sounding claim that objects have accidents, qualities, relations, and moments, it will also insist on the paradox that the object both has and does not have these terms.

2

Sensual Objects

Among the greatest philosophical schools of the twentieth century is the phenomenology founded by Husserl and developed by Heidegger. A remarkable paradox lies at the heart of this movement. For although phenomenology calls for a return "to the things themselves," Husserl and Heidegger have both been accused of idealism. And true enough, both of these thinkers seem to make everything a matter of its accessibility to human beings; an external world beyond humans plays little role in their thinking. And yet there is a certain undeniably realist *flavor* to phenomenology that one cannot find in Berkeley or even Hegel. In Husserl's works we find descriptions of blackbirds, centaurs, and mailboxes. In Heidegger there is much attention to objects such as hammers or jugs, and to everyday scenes at parties and railway platforms. This suggests that the themes of objects and realism do not entirely overlap, since both Husserl and Heidegger are quietly committed to objects despite their lack of full-blown realism.

While Husserl is often dismissed as just another idealist, he is in fact a zoological oddity among philosophers: an *object-oriented* idealist. Although Husserl remains confined to the intentional realm, he also discovers a fascinating rift within that realm: a gulf between objects and their qualities. The trees and blackbirds we encounter are not detailed presentations of specific bundles of qualities before the mind. Instead, intentional objects have a unified essential core surrounded by a swirling surface of accidents. In Heidegger's case we have a different situation: a genuine taste of the real world lying beyond the intentional sphere. In his tool-analysis we find real hammers and drills withdrawing from direct human access. If Husserl openly gives us intentional objects polarized between their accidents and their essential qualities, Heidegger tacitly gives us this same polarization for *real* objects. This chapter and the next will explain what I mean by "polarity" for each of the two philosophers.

A. Immanent Objectivity

Although phenomenology calls for a return to the things themselves, it paradoxically considers them only insofar as they appear. Since every form of idealism performs this same gesture on behalf of appearance, it might seem unoriginal at first. But we will see that Husserl adds a compelling twist to the problem. It is well known that phenomenology suspends the external world from consideration, refusing to accept any natural or causal theories about things. If I hear a siren in the night, then what I hear is a *siren*, not the transmission of sound waves through space leading to the vibration of my eardrums. All of this remains mere theory, while phenomenology limits us to that which is directly accessible. In *Ideas* I,[9] Husserl goes so far as to exclude all possibility of objects that are unobservable in principle by consciousness, and thus his drift towards idealism is complete. But even within the limits of this idealism, an unexpected attention to *objects* can be found from the start. Husserl's brilliant and charismatic mentor, Franz Brentano, had renovated the medieval doctrine of intentionality. What distinguishes the mental from the physical for Brentano is that mental acts are always directed toward an object. When I judge there is something judged; when I love there is something or someone loved. In directing my attention toward this something, I "intend" it. But that which I intend lies within consciousness, not outside it. Existing only on the interior of my experience, it is described by Brentano as "intentional inexistence" or "immanent objectivity." Husserl will push this immanent objectivity beyond Brentano's own understanding of it.

By placing any independent natural world outside of philosophy, Husserl pays a terrible price; his bracketing of the natural world is a brutally idealist gesture. In vain do his disciples protest that consciousness is never an isolated entity but always already outside itself through its intentional acts of observing, judging, hating, and loving. For in phenomenology these objects have no autonomy from consciousness. Their existence is already threatened if I shift my attention, fall asleep, or die, and all the more so if all rational beings in the universe were exterminated. A Husserlian might respond to these scenarios by claiming that the *essence* of these objects would endure even after the death of all thinking creatures. But even this response would miss the point: the things would still have no autonomous reality apart from being the objects of actual or potential observation. They are granted no secret life or inherent causal power, but are "real" only insofar as they might now or someday appear to consciousness. But unless objects are granted reality apart from such appearance, it is pointless to say that humans are always already engaged with things rather than being isolated minds, or that they are passive participants in an event rather than active constitutors of the world. Husserl's intentional realm has nothing real about it, nothing autonomous from an observer.

This problem with Husserl is widely known. His reward for paying this price can be found in his admirable ability to treat perceptions as genuine realities rather than annihilating them in favor of their physical or neural underpinnings. But this is true of all philosophies that grant some existence to the immanent realm; what makes Husserl unique is the unexpected drama he discovers there. Whereas Brentano focused solely on the immanent life of the mind, some of his students tried to supplement this immanence through reference to an outside world. This occurs most lucidly in the treatise of his Polish student Kasimir Twardowski, *On the Content and Object of*

Presentations.[10] This sparkling little work was received by the young Husserl in a spirit of rivalry, with a revealing mixture of admiration and disdain. For Twardowski, a doubling occurs: there is an *object* lying outside the mind and a *content* inside it. Much attention has been paid to Husserl's rejection of this claim. He famously holds that the Berlin intended in consciousness and the Berlin existing in the world are one and the same,[11] and this sentiment paves the way for his increasing idealism over the years. What is less often noticed, though it lies at the heart of Husserl's breakthrough, is the fact that he does not simply reject Twardowski's distinction between object and content. Instead, he imports it into the heart of the immanent realm itself.

Brentano had said relatively little about objects, and emphasized instead that all conscious acts are rooted in *presentations*. Something must be presented to the mind before it can be judged, hated, or loved. While Twardowski augmented this model by introducing a real object beyond the presentations, Husserl's rejection of such doubling might seem to place him on the side of Brentano. But this is not the case. For in the *Logical Investigations* Husserl openly modifies Brentano's model, saying that consciousness is not formed of presentations, but of *object-giving acts*. And this difference is no trivial subtlety. For in any presentation all qualitative details are on exactly the same footing. All are equally part of the presentation: the lofty ascent of the tree is no more a part of it than the exact position of each individual leaf. In this way consciousness is made up of "bundles of content," and we remain within the bounds of British Empiricism. For Husserl, by contrast, not everything in consciousness is equal. Even while confining us to the immanent sphere of consciousness, he borrows Twardowski's distinction between object and content for use *within* this sphere. Retreating into the phenomenal world like a monk into the desert, what he finds is a previously unsuspected fault line in the world.

B. Adumbrations

Let there be no doubt: the phenomenal world for Husserl is not made up only of specific content, as Brentano and Twardowski both hold. Instead, the Husserlian phenomenal realm is torn apart by a duel between objects and the content through which they are manifest. Recall what happens in any phenomeno-logical analysis. Perhaps Husserl circles a water tower at a distance of one hundred meters, at dusk, in a state of suicidal depression. As he moves along his sad path while observing the tower, it constantly shows different profiles. In each moment he will experience new details, but without the tower becoming a new tower in each instant. Instead, the tower is a unified "inten-tional object" that remains the same despite being presented through the greatest variety of different perceptions. The tower is always encountered through a specific profile: an *Abschattung* or "adumbration," as Husserl calls them. But these adumbra-tions are not the same thing as the intentional objects they manifest. If Husserl increases his circuit around the tower to three hundred meters at dawn in a mood of euphoria, it still seems to him like the same tower as yesterday evening. The object always remains the same despite numerous constant changes in its content. But unlike Twardowski's model, in which the object-pole is an anchor lying entirely outside consciousness, for Husserl both the object and content are immanent. It is true that Husserl denies this, but only because he accepts no "transcendent" world that would make phenomena "immanent" by contrast.

A point worth stressing is that the intentional object is no bundle of adumbrations. We do not grasp a tree or mailbox by seeing it from every possible side — which is physically, mentally, and perhaps logically impossible. The object is attained not by adding up its possible appearances to us, but by *subtracting* these adumbrations. That dog on the horizon need not have its hind leg raised exactly as it now does, nor does it cease to be the same dog if it stops growling and wags its tail in a spirit of welcome. Intentional objects always appear in more specific fashion than necessary, frosted over with accidental features that can be removed without the object itself changing identity for us. Here already we see Husserl's departure from empiricism. Just as an apple is not the sum total of its red, slippery, cold, hard, and sweet features in any given moment, it is also not the sum total of angles and distances from which it can be perceived. By contrast, Merleau-Ponty relapses into saying that the being of the house is "the house viewed from everywhere,"[12] while even Heidegger has little sense of the difference between intentional objects and their qualities.

Despite this difference between the unified object and its myriad qualities, we must avoid the error of thinking that Husserl's intentional object is somehow *concealed* from us. His great heir Heidegger has much to say about the veiling of things, and we will cover this point in detail in the chapters that follow. But by contrast, there is really no concealment for Husserl at all. Husserl's point is not that we only encounter adumbrations of trees, dogs, blackbirds, and mailboxes while the unified objects themselves remain hidden from us; that would be more like Heidegger or even Twardowski. Instead, according to Husserl we encounter the intentional object directly in experience from the start, expending our energy in taking it seriously. In the Husserlian framework, if I observe a distant mailbox from a hilltop under ominous lighting conditions, the mailbox is not "hidden" from me in the Heideggerian manner. Instead it is always present, but merely covered with the gems, glitter, and confetti of extraneous detail. The mailbox is not built up as a bundle of perceptually discrete shapes and colors, or even from tiny pixels of sense experience woven together by habit. Instead, shapes and colors belong from the outset to the unified mailbox. Husserl's breakthrough in philosophy has not been fully assimilated if we neglect his revolutionary distinction within the sensual realm between unified objects and their shifting multitude of features. These features are no less subordinated to their objects than are satellites to the gravity of the earth. For Husserl unlike Brentano, consciousness is not made up of definite presentations, but of object-giving acts. For this reason, any comparison between Husserl and Heidegger on this point is misguided. In Husserl we find that objects are not withdrawn from human access, but all too heavily adorned with frivolous decorations and surface-effects.

The metaphysics presented in this book lays great stress on several key tensions between objects and their qualities. There turn out to be four such tensions, and we have just met with the first of them. The phenomenal realm is not only an idealist prison cut off from access to the outer world. Rather, it displays a tension between intentional objects and their ever-shifting qualities. But due to the antiseptic sterility of the term "intentional," I propose to speak instead of *sensual* objects as a synonymous phrase. Nor is sterility the only reason for avoiding the phrase 'intentional objects.' Too much confusion has arisen over this famous term: many analytic philosophers believe that intentional objects are those lying outside human consciousness, even though both Brentano and Husserl mean it in a purely immanent sense. Thus, the phrase 'sensual objects' is more effective at conveying that we do not speak here of the real world beyond human access where only real objects belong. In all phenomenal experience, there is a tension between sensual objects and their sensual qualities. The ocean remains the same though its successive waves advance and recede. A Caribbean parrot retains its identity no matter how exactly its wings currently flap, and no matter what curses or threats it now utters in the Spanish language. The phenomenal world is not just an idealist sanctuary from the blows of harsh reality, but an active seismic zone where intentional objects grind slowly against their own qualities.

C. Eidetic Features

Yet it turns out that Husserl's sensual objects are involved in two tensions or polarizations, not just one. We have already seen a first rift within the phenomenal sphere, which lies between the sensual object and those swirling accidental qualities that encrust its surface like jewels or dust. Yet this cannot be the only polarization in which sensual objects are involved. After all, if we strip away the swirling accidents of an object, what remains is not merely an empty pole of unity. The sensual dog, pine tree, and lighthouse are different objects not just because their shifting accidents are different. By stripping away this surface noise through Husserl's method of eidetic variation, what we attain is not the same featureless unity for every sensual object — a "bare particular," in the terms of analytic philosophy. Instead, we approach what Husserl calls the *eidos* of an object. This second tension is a bit stranger than the first. In one sense the tensions an object undergoes with its own accidents and its own eidetic features are similar, since in both cases the object is not assembled from a bundle of qualities. We cannot construct a mailbox by piling up essential qualities any more than by piling up outward profiles. The object is one; its qualities are many, whether they be accidental or eidetic. Hence in both directions there is a difference between the object and its multitude of traits. Yet there are other respects in which the two tensions are markedly different. For in the first place the object does not need its accidents, which can be shifted nearly at will without affecting the character of the object. Yet the same is obviously not true of its essential features, which the object desperately needs in order to be what it is. And in the second place, the accidental qualities lie directly before us in experience, but the eidetic ones do not. Late in the *Logical Investigations*, Husserl makes it clear that the eidos of an object is incapable of sensual presence; we have access to it only through so-called categorial intuition, such that only the work of the intellect delivers the eidos. But in fact, there is no reason to assume that the intellect can make reality directly present in a way that the senses cannot. Whether my hands or my intellect alerts me to the electrical conductivity of copper, neither sensing nor knowing is what conducts electricity throughout the world. In other words, Husserl is wrong to distinguish between the sensual and the intellectual here; both sensual and categorial intuition are forms of intuition, and to intuit something is not the same as to be it. Hence the eidetic features of any object can never be made present even through the intellect, but can only be approached indirectly by way of allusion, whether in the arts or in the sciences. Copper wires, bicycles, wolves, and triangles all have real qualities, but these genuine traits will never be exhausted by the feeble sketches of them delivered to our hearts and minds. A proton or volcano must have a variety of distinct properties, but these remain just as withdrawn from us as the proton and volcano themselves.

What we have here is the strange case of a sensual object with *real* qualities. For the qualities of its eidos are necessary for it to exist, but are also withdrawn from all access, and "real" is the only possible name for such a feature. Now, we might easily say that the sensual object both has and does not have its accidental features, since the exact profile of a house at dusk is somehow attached to the house without being necessary for it. But somewhat surprisingly, the same is true even of an object's eidetic features. Here too it both has and does not have them, since it is always green, hard, or slippery in its own specific way, and is not built up out of these traits. Just like the accidental qualities, the eidetic qualities are imbued from the start with the reality or style of the object to which they belong.

It should already be clear that Husserl's suspension of the outer world has a positive side no less than a negative one. Though it will be necessary to reject his flattening of reality onto a phenomenal surface, and even to reject his undue exclusion of inanimate entities from the ranks of entities that can encounter phenomena, his sensual realm already raises interesting problems for the metaphysics of objects. In Husserl's hands, sensual objects are no longer two-dimensional apparitions trapped in the human mind: instead, everything from black-birds, mailboxes, and trees to centaurs, numbers, and wishes becomes the site of two simultaneous polarizations. The sensual object is something less than its sensual qualities, since these superfluous additions can be scraped away without affecting the underlying sensual object. But the sensual object is something less than its real qualities as well, since it deploys these qualities only in a certain specific way. On the one hand we have the sensual object and its sensual qualities, half-welded together in experience. But on the other hand, to articulate what makes this particular parrot be what it is requires an analysis of real qualities that can only be hinted at allusively or obliquely by the intellect without ever becoming nakedly present.

Terminologically, we can speak of the "encrustation" of qualities on the surface of a sensual object. Any sensual object is always encountered in a more detailed form than necessary: this city skyline need not be glimmering in its exact current way in order to be recognized as this very skyline. But when speaking of the real qualities that a sensual object must possess in order to be what it is, it is not a matter of encrustation, but of what might be called "submergence." The necessary qualities of a sensual object are sunk beneath its surface like the hull of a Venetian galley, invisible to the observer who is dazzled by the flags and emblems covering the ship, or the music played on its deck by captive singers and drummers. Though the hull is submerged, it remains vital for the seaworthiness of the ship. By analogy, the real qualities of the sensual object can only be inferred indirectly rather than witnessed. The sensual object cannot exist without having both sorts of qualities simultane-ously. It would not be a sensual object if it did not somehow appear, but would also not be this very sensual object if it did not have the specific eidetic features that make it so. But one important clarification must be made. Husserl speaks of real qualities in generic terms, such that a certain shade of green can be embodied in many different particular objects; the same holds for the "eternal objects" of Whitehead, and for most other thinkers who have dealt with the topic of essence. By contrast, qualities as described in this book are always individualized by the object to which they belong. To put it in the terms of analytic philosophy, they are "tropes." But in any case, the sensual object is not merely an idealist illusion, but the site of two crucial polarizations in the cosmos.

D. Summary

As a rule, realist philosophers are satisfied to claim that there is more to things than our representations of them. Consciousness may be filled with manifest images, but these are not primary; instead, these images are generated or produced by realities that are not themselves manifest. In our time most realists are committed to scientific naturalism, and hold that the natural world has primacy over human images of it. In this way they attack the notion that conscious experience is the starting point of philosophy, and undermine it by grounding philosophy in the deeper natural things that give rise to such experience. But notice that this is merely the undermining flip side of mainstream idealism, which overmines objects by saying that they are nothing more than their manifestation in experience. What typical realists and typical idealists share is a tendency to skip the intermediate level of objects altogether. They say either that there is a basic layer of natural elements that explains all objects, or that objects are nothing more than bundles of traits that are directly manifest to the observer. What makes Husserl so special among idealists is his discovery of objects *within* the phenomenal sphere. Despite being an idealist, he *feels* like a realist to such a degree that his followers often assume there is no more reality to be had than the kind that Husserl already addresses. Husserl is in fact the first *object-oriented* idealist. He knows the painful and seductive labor needed to look beyond the specific traits through which an object is manifest. By contrast, such authors as Berkeley or Fichte pay no attention at all to the duel between mailboxes and their various sparkling and shifting features. Nor is it thinkable that Fichte would ever imagine circling a tree from various distances and angles in different moods. But for Husserl this procedure cannot be avoided: the sensual object cannot be assembled from its current observable features or even its sum total of possible profiles.

At the risk of repetition, it is useful to summarize what we have learned from Husserl. For him the natural world outside the mind is excluded from the starting point of philosophy, since its suppositions are merely theories. We cannot begin by thinking that a mailbox is made of pieces of sheet metal with various chemical properties, or of atoms, quarks, electrons, or strings. By the same token we cannot view either mailboxes or humans as created entities in contrast with a transcendent creator. All we know initially is that objects are phenomena present in consciousness. In our conscious life we intend these objects; as Brentano already knew, perception is perception *of something*, and the same holds true for judgments, wishes, and acts of love and hate. But whereas Brentano claimed that all intentional life is grounded in presentations, Husserl noted that consciousness is not a flatland in which everything is on the same footing. Instead of presentations there are object-giving acts, which means that we must distinguish between sensual objects as unvarying inner cores and all their countless manifestations. The various trees and centaurs encountered in conscious life are simply trees and centaurs, and are not bound up with the superfluity of details through which they are always encountered.

In this way Husserl discovers a tension between object and content *within* the sensual realm — a great fault line that tears phenomena in half from the start. Sensual objects are different from all the sensual accidents through which they appear. But these sensual objects are not empty poles of unity that differ from each other only due to the specific colors, angles, moods, and lighting conditions through which they appear. Even if we could strip away all the accidental features of horses, dogs, and chairs, these objects would still differ from each other. Each object has *eidetic* features no less than accidental ones. Normally, we have only a vague sense of the exact character of the dog lying behind the numerous facile encrustations with which it appears. The work of theoretical consciousness is to articulate the features of that dog, to unlock its eidos. Yet we have seen that despite Husserl's belief that adequate intuition into the eidos of a thing is possible, this eidos is made up of *real* qualities. Hence, access to them can only be indirect and allusive, which rules out any direct access to them of either sensual or intellectual type. The real qualities of the palm tree do not resemble our lists of these qualities any more than the palm tree itself resembles the one we see. Real qualities withdraw from direct access no less than real objects do. In this way the sensual object serves as the crossroads for two crucial tensions in the cosmos: sensual object vs. its sensual qualities, and sensual object vs. its real qualities. And this intersection is the great discovery of Husserl, ignored by more recent authors who treat him as already passé, or who mistake him for an arid technical maestro.

Nonetheless, Husserl remains an idealist. His objects are incapable of doing anything other than appearing in consciousness. Indeed, without consciousness they are incapable of existing at all: whether that consciousness belongs to me, another thinking being, or at least some *possible* thinking being. Even an object-oriented idealist like Husserl cannot do justice to objects; his objects are of the purely sensual variety, deprived of autonomous reality or action beyond the kingdom of the mind. Now, as a general rule the most dangerous philosophical problems are those that we falsely believe we have already overcome. In such cases the constant thorn in the flesh of an unsolved problem disappears, and one side of a paradox is chosen at the expense of the other while denying that this has even occurred. And the unfortunate truth is that phenomenology has always been guilty of a sin of this kind. For as much as phenomenology claims to stand somewhere beyond the supposed "pseudo-problem" of realism and idealism, it falls squarely on the idealist side of the idealist dispute.

Amidst this paradoxical situation of a philosophy that is both idealist and object-oriented, the music of Martin Heidegger was first heard rising in the distance. His drastic reformation of phenomenology was enough to make him perhaps the greatest philosopher of the twentieth century. There are shortcomings to be found in Heidegger, as in every major thinker. But if there is

FIGURE 1: Two Tensions in Sensual Objects (Husserl)

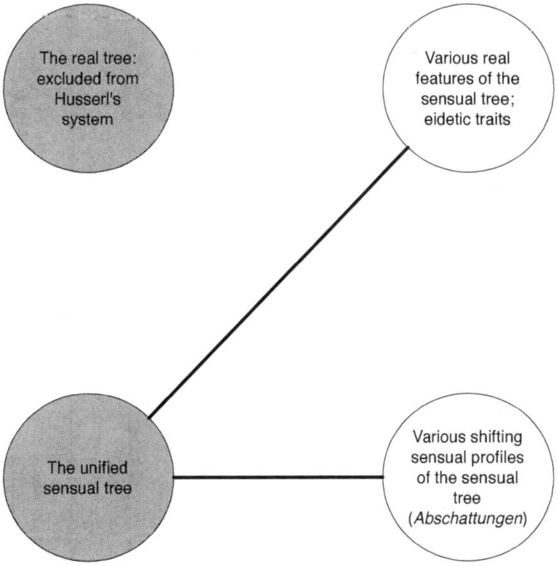

one error that he does avoid, it is surely Husserl's confinement within the sensual sphere. While it is true that Heidegger leaves *Sein* and *Dasein* in a permanent, mutually dependent couple, this does not entail that being is exhausted by its manifestation to humans. In Heidegger, there are real objects to go along with the sensual ones.

3

Real Objects

In the eyes of many, Heidegger is the major philosopher of the twentieth century; he is certainly the major influence on the metaphysics presented in this book. For these reasons he will be the subject of extensive treatment in the coming chapters. So far we have considered Husserl's contribution to our topic. Despite his idealism, Husserl describes a tension that is foreign to most idealists between the sensual objects we encounter and their two kinds of traits: sensual and real. While this insight adds significant conflict and texture to an otherwise misty ideal realm, it still supposes a world in which the reality of objects does not exceed their presence to a conscious observer. For Heidegger the situation is different: if Husserl is a philosopher of presence, then Heidegger is a thinker of absence. His famous tool-analysis in *Being and Time* shows that our usual way of dealing with things is not observing them as present-at-hand (*vorhanden*) in consciousness, but silently relying on them as ready-to-hand (*zuhanden*). Hammers and drills are usually present to us only when they fail. Prior to this they withdraw into a subterranean background, enacting their reality in the cosmos without appearing in the least. Insofar as they recede into the depths, tool-beings tend to coalesce into a *system* of equipment in which it is difficult to distinguish between individual beings. This has the undermining implication that the multiplicity of beings belongs to a derivative level of presence, with priority given to a deeper and unified system of reference.

But this is a misunderstanding of Heidegger's discovery, even if it sometimes afflicts Heidegger himself. The tool-analysis does not give us a monistic lump of being, but a landscape where individual objects are withdrawn into private interiors, barely able to relate at all. Contrary to all appearances, Heidegger is an object-oriented thinker no less than Husserl. The key difference is that he replaces Husserl's sensual objects with his own unique model of *real* ones. But these real objects complement sensual objects rather than replacing them.

A. The Tool-Analysis

Heidegger radicalizes phenomenology from within. Stirred into action by the writings of Brentano and Husserl, the young Heidegger came to be viewed as the crown prince of phenomenology, and eventually as a traitor to the movement. Husserl's philosophical method is to bracket all consideration of the outside world and focus solely on the phenomena that appear to consciousness. His rebellious heir Heidegger reverses this procedure, drawing our attention to what lies behind all phenomena. He does this not in order to restore scientific naturalism to the throne, but to give us the sense of a reality much weirder than any that science has known. Heidegger's palace revolt against phenomenology is most visible in his famous tool-analysis, first published in *Being and Time*,[13] but already found in his earliest Freiburg lecture course in 1919.[14] The tool-analysis is probably the greatest moment in the philosophy of the past century: a thought experiment comparable in power to Plato's myth of the cave. If Husserl's mission is to suspend all theories of the natural world in favor of a detailed survey of conscious experience, Heidegger's philosophy is a sweeping campaign against presence: whether it be presence to the mind or to anything else. If we pursue this campaign with an intensity that Heidegger never attempted, we soon arrive at the borderlands of a speculative philosophy closed off to the great thinker himself.

Heidegger's tool-analysis is familiar to anyone even loosely acquainted with recent philosophy. At any moment I am conscious of a number of objects lying before me: desk, lamp, computer, telephone. Yet Heidegger notes that most of the things with which we contend are not explicitly present to the mind at all, but have the mode of being of "equipment," or readiness-to-hand. These range from the eyeglasses that I usually fail to notice, to the beating heart that keeps me alive, to the chair and solid floor that prevent me from toppling to the earth, to the grammatical structures mastered in earliest childhood. Conscious awareness makes up only a tiny portion of our lives. For the most part, objects withdraw into a shadowy subterranean realm that supports our conscious activity while seldom erupting into view. Heidegger also frequently claims that this occluded underground realm is a unified system rather than a collection of autonomous objects: strictly speaking, there is no such thing as "an" equipment, since tools are reciprocally and globally determined by their mutual references. It should also be noted that despite the use of words such as "equipment" and "tool," Heidegger is not describing a limited taxonomy of one specific kind of entity as opposed to others. It is not just an analysis of hammers, drills, knives, and forks, but of everything. For all entities tend to reside in a cryptic background rather than appearing before the mind.

The tool-analysis first occurs in Heidegger's 1919 Freiburg lecture course, with its embarrassing fantasia of a "Senegal Negro" who misinterprets classroom furniture as protection from arrows and slingstones.[15] But the first published appearance of the analysis is found eight years later, beginning with Section 15 of *Being and Time*. Against the claim that the world is filled with objective material things that are later supplemented with values and psychological projections, Heidegger treats tool-being itself as the primordial nature of things. "We shall call those entities which we encounter in concern *'equipment.'*"[16] And while Heidegger claims that we deal with equipment by means of a kind of "sight" (*Sicht*) that he calls "circumspection" (*Umsicht*), this supposed sight does not make the tools visible in the least. For what is most typical of these tools as "ready-to-hand" is as follows: "The ready-to-hand is not grasped thematically at all.... The peculiarity of what is proximally ready-to-hand is that, in its readiness-to-hand, it must, as it were, withdraw in order to be ready-to-hand quite authentically."[17] In short, insofar as the tool is a tool, it is quite invisible. And what makes it invisible is the way that it disappears in favor of some purpose that it serves: "Equipment is essentially something 'in-order-to'.... In the 'in-order-to' as a structure there lies an *assignment* or *reference* of something to something." And furthermore: "Equipment — in accordance with its equipmentality — always is *in terms of* its belonging to other equipment: ink-stand, pen, ink, paper, blotting pad, table, lamp, furniture, windows, doors, room."[18] For Heidegger tools do not exist as isolated entities. Indeed, their very contours are designed with other entities in mind: "A covered railway platform takes account of bad weather; an installation for public lighting takes account of the darkness, or rather of specific changes in the presence or absence of daylight — the 'position of the sun'."[19] Instead of thinking that extra-mental reality is founded on what appears to consciousness, we must join Heidegger in concluding the opposite, while also agreeing with him that what withdraws from consciousness are not lumps of objective physical matter. Instead, the world in itself is made of realities withdrawing from all conscious access.

Then contra Husserl, the usual manner of things is not to appear as phenomena, but to withdraw into an unnoticed subterranean realm. Heidegger says that we generally notice equipment only when it somehow fails. An earthquake calls my attention to the solid ground on which I rely, just as medical problems alert me to the bodily organs on which I silently depend. But entities need not "break" in the literal sense of the term, as if due to failing bolts, wires, or engines. For there is already a failure of sorts when I simply turn my attention towards entities, reflecting consciously on my bodily organs or the solid floor of my home. But even when I do so, these things themselves are not yet within my grasp. There will always be aspects of these phenomena that elude me; further surprises might always be in store. No matter how hard I work to become conscious of things, environing conditions still remain of which I never become fully aware. When I stare at a river, wolf, government, machine, or army, I do not grasp the whole of their reality. This reality slips from view into a perpetually veiled underworld, leaving me with only the most frivolous simulacra of these entities. In short, the phenomenal reality of things for consciousness does not use up their being. The readiness-to-hand of an entity is not exhaustively deployed in its presence-at-hand.

The implications of the tool-analysis are far weightier than readers of Heidegger usually imagine. This claim will be developed over the next several chapters, but one key point is already clear. We have seen that ready-to-hand and present-at-hand do not give us a taxonomy of different *kinds* of objects; they are not two limited regions of entities among many others. Instead, tool and broken tool make up the whole of Heidegger's universe. He recognizes these two basic modes of being, and *only* these two: entities withdraw into a silent underground while also exposing themselves to presence. This is certainly true of pitchforks, shovels, knives, tunnels, and bridges, which invisibly perform their labors while also sometimes existing as phenomenal images before the mind. But it is also true of entities not usually regarded as "tools": for even colors, shapes, and numbers all have a reality that is not fully exhausted by the exact way in which a thinker considers them. Such entities are locked into a global dualism between ready-to-hand and present-at-hand no less than wooden or metallic hardware are. And despite Heidegger's denials, even human Dasein partakes of both modes of being. For even if Dasein is not "used" in the same way as a rubber hose, it still displays the same two sides as any other entity. Even humans withdraw into a dark reality that is never fully understood, while also being present to observers from the outside.

B. Beyond Theory and Praxis

One typical reading of the tool-analysis is to view it as a form of pragmatism. It is easy to see why this happens. Husserl can be viewed as a philosopher of patient theoretical description of the phenomena, aiming at a best-case scenario of adequate intuition into the essence of things. By contrast, Heidegger has no hope that theory can do justice to the things. Theory is secondary for him, and thus might seem to arise only from an unnoticed background of pre-theoretical practices. Instead of granting priority to a lucid conscious observer, Heidegger sees human Dasein as thrown into a context that is taken for granted long before it ever becomes present to the mind. Consciousness is reduced to a tiny corner of reality, while practical handling and coping become central to his model of the world. Invisible praxis is the soil from which all theory emerges. In this way, Heidegger is depicted as a pragmatist. It is often added that John Dewey noticed the same point three decades earlier, and hence (at least in America) Heidegger is sometimes portrayed as just a tardy pragmatist whose tool-analysis teaches us nothing that was not already described by others. If Heidegger has any point of true originality, it is claimed, then this must be found in his tens of thousands of pages of historical writings. As an ontologist, he merely repeats the breakthroughs of pragmatism.

Despite my opposition to the pragmatist interpretation of Heidegger, this trend does have certain institutional merits. After all, the Anglo-American world remains dominated by analytic philosophy, an intellectual current in which pragmatism now enjoys great prestige. The abundance of pragmatist interpretations of Heidegger has at least succeeded in shifting his image among analytic philosophers from "unintelligible poet and pompous mystic" to "non-mentalist verificationist anti-realist," or something along the same lines. The most prominent analytic reader of Heidegger in America is surely Hubert Dreyfus, but someone more useful for our purposes is Mark Okrent, whose book *Heidegger's Pragmatism*[20] expresses more open support for the interpretation in question. For Okrent, "being" does not stand alone on the mountaintop of Heideggerian terminology; it is joined there by the term "understanding." For Okrent, "understanding" means practical know-how. As he describes Heidegger's position: "to understand x (for example, a hammer) is primarily to understand how to do y with x (to hammer) or how to use x (to use x as a hammer)."[21] Yet Okrent also claims that such understanding is ubiquitous, not episodic: understanding occurs *at all times* and *towards everything*. Yet as Okrent realizes, this seems to contradict the evident fact that humans are often perplexed by what they encounter, failing to understand it at all. His remedy for this paradox is to say that what humans ultimately understand are not the hammers, electrons, and dolphins they encounter, but rather *themselves*. "Heidegger doesn't claim that there can be no intention directed toward a thing unless we understand it. Rather, he asserts that one can't intend oneself, and that one can't intend anything else [either] unless one understands oneself."[22] This leads Okrent to a strange position, not rare among pragmatist readers of Heidegger, in which the outside world must be treated pragmatically, but the inner world is accessible to absolute transcendental knowledge, *even though* understanding of the outside world is also supposed to be just a variant of self-understanding. The contradiction is glaring, but there is no need to give a full critique of Okrent's book here. I will simply quote his conclusion about Heidegger, since it is so typical of pragmatist interpreters of this philosopher. For just like Rorty, Okrent does not see Heidegger as especially original: "With the possible exception of the emphasis on temporality, the principal doctrines of the early Heidegger concerning the primarily practical character of intentionality are hardly unique in the twentieth century. A whole series of philosophers, including John Dewey, the late Wittgenstein, and the contemporary American neo-pragmatists.... have made very similar points."[23]

But however popular it may currently be, the pragmatist reading of Heidegger misses the target. For the tool-analysis teaches us something much deeper than the emergence of conscious awareness from the prior unconscious use of things. In the first place, despite the etymology of the terms, it is wrong to identify the ready-to-hand with "practice" and the present-at-hand with "theory." To oppose the arrogant pretensions of theory, the tool-analysis shows us that the being of an apple, hammer, dog, or star is not exhausted by its presence in consciousness. No sensual profile of these things will ever exhaust its full reality, which withdraws into the dusk of a shadowy underworld. But if something hides behind the many profiles of an apple, what hides from view is not our *use* of the apple, but rather the apple itself. After all, using a thing distorts its reality no less than making theories about it does. If we unconsciously stand on a floor that has not yet broken, this standing relies on just a handful of qualities of the floor: its hardness or sturdiness, for instance. Our use of the floor as "equipment for standing" makes no contact with the abundance of extra qualities that dogs or mosquitoes might be able to detect. In short, both theory *and* practice are equally guilty of reducing things to presence-at-hand. It is true that some things are consciously in mind while others are unconsciously used. Yet the basic opposition in the tool-analysis is not between conscious and unconscious. Instead, the truly important rift lies between the withdrawn reality of any object and the distortion of that object by way of both theory *and* practice. Staring at a hammer does not exhaust its being, but neither does using it.

Yet there is still another way in which the difference between *vorhanden* and *zuhanden* is often misread. We are told that objects in consciousness appear as isolated abstractions, each existing on its own. Supposedly, the tool-analysis shows that entities themselves are not isolated, but belong to a total system in which each thing gains its meaning from its references to the others. Heidegger himself says that there is no such thing as "an" equipment, and this seems to make him an ontologist of relations. It is easy to see why this notion arises. A knife obviously has a very different reality when used in a restaurant kitchen, at a wedding banquet, or in a grisly triple homicide. But as convincing as it might sound, this reading of Heidegger misses the point. There is no real opposition between an isolated knife in consciousness and an invisibly used knife that belongs to a system. For whether the knife is seen or used, in both cases it is treated only in relation to something else, not in its own right.

It is certainly true that tools belong to a system. A flock of crows caged in a zoo is less ominous than the same flock hovering over a snowy field, and this in turn is less disturbing than the same group of crows when found in the corridors of a hospital. In this respect, entities seem to exist in reciprocal determination with one another, gaining their significance from neighboring entities, and it is easy to see why some might adopt a holistic view of equipment. But the same problem arises here as with the pragmatist reading of Heidegger. For although we might say that the different parts of a machine refer to and mutually determine one another, this mutual interrelation does not exhaust the reality of these parts. Insofar as tools belong to a system, they are already nothing but caricatures of themselves, reduced to presence-at-hand. And while it might seem that an isolated knife or window in consciousness is viewed in abstract isolation, even these images exist in a system, since they exist only in relation with the person who observes them. In short, both theoretical abstraction and the use of tools are equally guilty of distorting the tools themselves. Insofar as a tool is "used," it is no less present-at-hand than an image in consciousness. But a tool is not "used"; *it is*. And insofar as it is, the tool is not exhausted by its relations with human theory *or* human praxis.

C. Anti-Copernicus

In claiming that praxis distorts the reality of things no less than theory does, we make an important modification to Heidegger's tool-analysis. Given his proclaimed interest in Being itself rather than the various events of human existence, it is a modification he might well accept. Yet we are now on the verge of a more radical modification to which he would never agree. For if the being of things lies veiled behind all theory and practice, this is not due to some precious merit or defect of human Dasein, but to the fact that *all* relations translate or distort that to which they relate: even inanimate relations. When fire burns cotton, it makes contact only with the flammability of this material. Presumably fire does not interact at all with the cotton's odor or color, which are relevant only to creatures equipped with the organs of sense. Though it is true that the fire can change or destroy these properties that lie outside its grasp, it does so indirectly: through the detour of some additional feature of the cotton that color, odor, and fire are all able to touch. The being of the cotton withdraws from the flames, even if it is consumed and destroyed. Cotton-being is concealed not only from phenomenologists and textile workers, but from all entities that come into contact with it. In other words, the withdrawal of objects is not some cognitive trauma that afflicts only humans and a few smart animals, but expresses the permanent inadequacy of any relation at all. If there is no way to make a hammer perfectly present to my thought or action, there is also no way to make cotton present to fire, or glass to raindrops. It cannot be denied that human experience is rather different from inanimate contact, and presumably richer and more complex. But that is not the point. The more relevant issue is whether the difference between human relations with paper and a flame's relation with paper is different in kind or only in degree. And for the purposes of Heidegger's tool-analysis, it turns out to be merely a matter of degree. Although Heidegger tries to establish a pivotal gulf between Being and human Dasein, what he gives us instead is a basic difference between reality and relation.

This cuts against the grain of Kant's Copernican Revolution, which still dominates philosophy in our time. Both Latour and Meillassoux have justly objected to Kant's analogy: whereas Copernicus drove the earth from the center of the cosmos and put it into motion, Kant restores humans to the center in a manner more reminiscent of Ptolemy. If I now use the phrase "Anti-Copernicus," this is directed not at Copernicus the astronomer, but at Kant the self-proclaimed Copernican philosopher. We might ask what is most typical of the Kantian position. It is surely not his theories of space and time or his doctrine of the categories, since few philosophers still adhere to these views and yet Kant continues to dominate mainstream philosophy anyway. It is not the notion of things-in-themselves lying beyond all experience, since his German Idealist heirs abolished this concept with little effect on Kant's stature. No, what is truly characteristic of Kant's position is that the human-world relation takes priority over all others. For even those who read Kant as a realist strongly believing in things-in-themselves must still admit that the role of these things for Kant is little more than to haunt human awareness with a specter of its finitude. And more importantly, nowhere does Kant pay serious attention to relations between these things-in-themselves. What is always at stake for him is the relation between human subject on one side and world on the other. Today this human-world duopoly is taken for granted and rarely called into question. Heidegger certainly does not question it, and in this respect he remains an unwitting Copernican, forever focused on the relation between Dasein and world, with nothing to say about the interaction of fire and cotton apart from all human observers.

The towering exception in recent philosophy, the greatest of recent Anti-Copernicans, is surely Alfred North Whitehead. This remarkable thinker abolished the Kantian prejudice by saying that all human and non-human entities have equal status insofar as they all *prehend* other things, relating to them in one way or another.[24] For Whitehead, unlike for Heidegger, the human-world coupling has no higher status than the duels between comets and planets, or dust and moonlight. All relations are on exactly the same footing. This does not entail a projection of human properties onto the non-human world, but rather the reverse: what it says is that the crude prehensions made by minerals and dirt are no less relations than are the sophisticated mental activity of humans. Instead of placing souls into sand and stones, we find something sandy or stony in the human soul.

Now, many philosophers claim to be realists despite upholding the Kantian duopoly of human and world. They think that to posit some unarticulated reality beyond experience is enough to escape idealism. Perhaps they are right; perhaps they do deserve the name of realists. But if that is the case, then there is little reason to be excited about realism. Against such claims, we should always observe the following litmus test: no philosophy does justice to the world unless it treats all relations as equally relations, which means as equally translations or distortions. Inanimate collisions must be treated in exactly the same way as human perceptions, even if the latter are obviously more *complicated* forms of relation. As soon as we do this, we have pushed Heidegger in the direction of metaphysics. Though his rejection of the term "metaphysics" is well known, he rejects it only in the form of ontotheology, in which one special kind of entity is viewed as the root of all others, and that is the opposite of my goal. Most importantly, we now have a theory in which rocks withdraw from windows no less than from human theory and praxis. Such a theory surely deserves the name of speculative metaphysics.

D. Two Tensions

There are moments when Heidegger tends to treat being as unified and to find multiplicity only in the kingdom of presence, just as we find in the early Levinas. That is to say, there are times when Heidegger equates any talk of multiple beings with talk of mere presence-at-hand. To discuss being itself means to move deeper than the *vorhanden*, and this entails an undermining of all specific beings. At other times, especially from 1949 onward, Heidegger is perfectly willing to allow specific beings to withdraw into shadow and *remain* specific rather than melting into a holistic global tool-system. But our goal is not to learn Heidegger's true opinion: his tool-analysis is a thought experiment, and here as in physics we are bound by the truth of the experiment more than by Heidegger's own personal views on it. What I have tried to show is that if we define an object through its role in a system of interrelations, objects are thereby undermined, reduced to the caricatured image they present to all other things. The only way to do justice to objects is to consider that their reality is free of all relation, deeper than all reciprocity. The object is a dark crystal veiled in a private vacuum: irreducible to its own pieces, and equally irreducible to its outward relations with other things.

In discussing Husserl we spoke of sensual objects. Such objects exist only for another object that encounters them, and are merely encrusted with accidental qualities rather than "hiding" behind them. By contrast, in Heidegger's tools we have *real* objects, which differ from the sensual ones in both respects.

First, the real object is autonomous from whatever encounters it. If I close my eyes to sleep or die, the sensual tree is vaporized, while the real tree continues to flourish even if all sentient beings are destroyed along with me. Second, though sensual objects always inhabit experience and are not hidden behind their qualities, real objects must always hide.

But despite these differences, there are important similarities between the two kinds of objects. Both are autonomous units. Both are irreducible to any bundle of traits, since they are able to withstand numerous changes in the qualities that belong to them. And most importantly, both real and sensual objects are polarized with two different kinds of qualities. We saw that a sensual object is encrusted at every moment with purely accidental sensual qualities, while beneath it are submerged the more crucial real features that belong to the eidos. The same two polarities are found in the case of real objects. For on the one

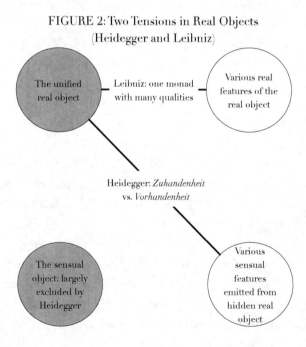

FIGURE 2: Two Tensions in Real Objects
(Heidegger and Leibniz)

The unified real object

Leibniz: one monad with many qualities

Various real features of the real object

Heidegger: *Zuhandenheit* vs. *Vorhandenheit*

The sensual object: largely excluded by Heidegger

Various sensual features emitted from hidden real object

hand the real hammer emits sensual qualities into the sphere of presence, despite being withdrawn in its own right. The qualities encountered in experience must somehow emanate from a real object no less than a sensual one, because even though such qualities are obviously attached to a sensual object in any given moment, they are the sole way in which the withdrawn tool-beings become present in consciousness. And on the other hand the real hammer is not a sheer empty unit, but has a multitude of real qualities of its own. This is clear from some remarks of Leibniz, who observes that even though each monad must be one monad, each also needs a multitude of qualities to be what it is, to differ from other monads rather than being interchangeable with them.[25]

This brief survey of Husserl and Heidegger has already given us the basic elements of an object-oriented metaphysics. The two great figures of phenomenology are united once and for all. While there may be an infinity of objects in the cosmos, they come in only two kinds: the real object that withdraws from all experience, and the sensual object that exists *only* in experience. And along with these we also have two kinds of qualities: the sensual qualities found in experience, and the real ones that Husserl says are accessible intellectually rather than through sensuous intuition. This yields four distinct poles in the universe. Normally, any group of four terms can be paired in six possible permutations — or ten permutations, if we allow for combinations of two of the same kind. But for now we focus only on those pairings that bring together an object-pole and a quality-pole. And of course there are only four such pairs: real object/real quality, sensual object/sensual quality, real object/sensual quality, and sensual object/real quality. In fact, we have already touched on all four cases, and they provide the major subject matter for the remainder of this book.

The pairing of sensual object with sensual quality is the first great discovery of Husserl, in which sensual objects are fully present, but always surrounded by a mist of accidental features and profiles. His second great discovery is the union of sensual objects with real qualities, since the phenomena in consciousness would be empty poles of unity unless they had some definite character, and this character is formed of the real eidetic qualities that can only be the target of intellectual and never sensuous intuition. The coupling of real objects with sensual qualities is the topic of Heidegger's tool-analysis, where a concealed subterranean hammer is somehow translated into sensual presence by means of a surface accessible to thought or action. Finally, the pairing of real objects with real qualities is what allows real objects to differ from one another rather than being empty unified substrata with no definite character. By developing this model in more detail, we will arrive at the doorstep of a new kind of philosophy.

FIGURE 3: The Fourfold Structure Emerges

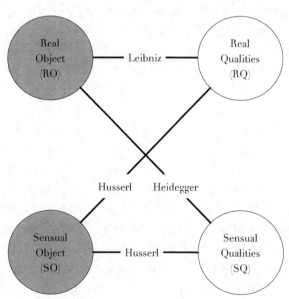

More on Heidegger

It is worth lingering a bit over Heidegger's contributions. Soon we will need to discuss his strange concept of *das Geviert*: the fourfold. But before moving on to that fascinating and perplexing topic, a few other points are of interest. First, it might be necessary to convince the reader further that the tool-analysis has a deeper sense than is usually believed, and that it does not merely oppose present-at-hand conscious images to ready-to-hand practical equipment. Second, I would also like to speak against the notion that Heidegger is a philosopher of time: for in fact he is a philosopher of isolated instants, though these instants are far more articulated than one usually believes. Third, this will lead us to the further result that Heidegger is a rather monotonous philosopher who has almost no other subject than the constant reversal between absence and presence, or tool and broken tool. Fourth and in closing, I will explain why I think Heidegger leads us to realism, and that the tool-analysis makes great contributions to overcoming the Copernican philosophy of human access. If all these things can be shown, we will have a rather different picture of Heidegger from the one that is widely accepted. Instead of a pragmatist, a philosopher of time, or a thinker who reduces reality to its accessibility to human Dasein, he emerges as a realist metaphysician focused intensely on the ambiguous state of specific instants.

A. Three Kinds of Presence
The previous chapter called for rejecting the usual view that readiness-to-hand refers to practical action. Praxis is not deep

enough to do justice to objects, just as theory is not. But in order to complete our transformation of Heidegger's tool-being, we should emphasize that his "presence-at-hand" has multiple meanings, and that all of these meanings ultimately refer to relationality. The typical reading of tools and presence for Heidegger, sometimes supported by the philosopher's own remarks, is that *vorhanden* refers to things in their supposed independence from humans, while *zuhanden* refers to things as wrapped up in human purposes. But in fact the opposite is the case: the ready-to-hand must always be independent, and the present-at-hand must be dependent. If tool-beings are worthy of greater esteem than the images in consciousness, this is not because they are more dependent on human Dasein, but the opposite. Any manner of reducing objects to their accessibility to us is a way of reducing them to presence-at-hand, and hence is something to be avoided. It is seldom noted that Heidegger uses "present-at-hand" to refer to several different kinds of situations, of which at least three come to mind. First, there is presence-at-hand in Husserl's sense, which refers to phenomena present to the mind. Second, there is the Heideggerian phenomenon of the broken tool that suddenly becomes present to us when it breaks or fails. But third and finally, there is the being of nature as disclosed by science. This is supposedly independent of humans, though in fact it is entirely dependent on our own scientific modeling of it.

The first sense of presence-at-hand, and the most important foil for Heidegger, is the "phenomenon" in Husserl's sense. By reducing a thing to its accessibility to consciousness, the thing itself is turned into a caricature, or "cut off at the knees" as the young Heidegger says. This is obviously true of perception as Husserl portrays it. But only to a certain extent is it true of Husserl's model of theoretical comportment. We recall his view that insight into the eidos of an object comes only from categorial intuition rather than the sensuous kind, and categorial intuition requires an oblique sort of access to reality rather than a direct one. But at least Husserl seems to think it possible that we might attain adequate intuition into things, and to this extent he is guilty of reducing things to presence in consciousness, whether he is speaking of perception or of theory. What makes the phenomena merely present-at-hand is the fact that they *appear* to us, and while Husserl regards this as a virtue, Heidegger knows it to be a terrible vice. The things themselves must have autonomy from their relation to us, or they are not the things themselves. We have seen further that the pragmatic handling of tools also belongs in this category, since this handling turns things into superficial caricatures no less than staring at them does. In short, what makes something present-at-hand is not that it is stationed in consciousness as a target of visual inspection, but that it is allowed to exist only in relation. But this is equally true of practical implements.

A second scenario that Heidegger describes as present-at-hand is that of the "broken tool," which no longer functions invisibly but now intrudes on our awareness. The broken lamp, desk, or hammer now lying before me are perhaps independent of my invisible practical activity, but in no way are they independent of me. On the contrary, all are now phenomena in consciousness. Given that the invisible tool in the midst of practical use should already be viewed as a kind of presence-at-hand, the same should be all the more true of the broken tool that obtrudes into view.

But what about the third case — nature? Here too, there is nothing the least bit independent about objects as defined by the natural sciences. Heidegger repeatedly reminds us that such objects are abstractions that reduce the things of the world to a set of present-at-hand traits that fail to capture the cryptic, withdrawn reality of the things. If we weigh and measure a thing, describe its physical properties, or note its objective position in space-time, these qualities hold good for the thing only insofar as it is relates to us or to something else. In short, the thing as portrayed by the natural sciences is the thing made dependent on our knowledge, and not in its untamed, subterranean reality. Heidegger more than anyone else is the one who has shown this. By contrast, the *Zuhandenheit* of entities is apparently bound up with human use, and Heidegger adds that tools are not isolated, but exist in a global system. Yet to accept this at face value is to take the word "tool" too literally, for we have seen that the tool-being of a thing withdraws not just from human theory and praxis, but from any relations at all. Any relation will be a translation or distortion of its terms. To this extent, insofar as a thing functions as a tool it is already present-at-hand, already reduced to its functional effects on humans or on neighboring tools. In other words, the opposition is not really between tools on one side and broken tools on the other, but between the withdrawn tool-being of things on one side and both broken and non-broken tools on the other. After all, the functioning pragmatic tool is present for human praxis just as the broken tool is present for human consciousness. And neither of these will suffice, because what we are looking for is the thing insofar as it *exists*, not insofar as it is present to either theory or praxis.

B. Temporality Without Time

Given that Heidegger's major work is entitled *Being and Time*, it is only natural to suppose that he has much to tell us about temporality. Time is the horizon of being, he says, and in other respects he does make time sound very important in his thinking. It is easy to imagine that instead of a rigid old-fashioned theory of substance, Heidegger is the champion of a self-differentiating being that is always in flux. This might seem especially evident given his constant critique of philosophies that reduce being to the present, along with those theological models that identify being with eternity. By contrast, Heidegger seems like the undeniable champion of temporal dynamism. Nonetheless, all of this is surprisingly misleading, since Heidegger actually has nothing whatsoever to tell us about time. His critique of presence is in fact not aimed at present instants as opposed to past and future times. Instead, it actually saves the present moment by showing that this very moment is already aflame with ambiguity, torn asunder in threefold fashion. Heidegger often criticizes the idea that time is "a sequence of now-points," and one can easily imagine Bergson making the same complaint. Yet it is interesting to note that the two thinkers would make this complaint for *opposite* reasons. For Bergson, the reason that time is not a sequence of now-points is because there is no such thing as an isolated now, no lonely cinematic frame distinct from all other frames. But for Heidegger the real problem with the sequence of now-points is not the nows, but the *sequence*. What he most dislikes is the idea that each moment of time would be a present-at-hand instant that would then disappear in favor of a later one. Instead, Heidegger thinks that the individual moment is already sufficiently intriguing to be worthy of detailed analysis. For him the structure of temporality has nothing to do with turning isolated now-points into a silky flow of time, but much to do with making the isolated instant more ambiguously fascinating than ever before.

It should always be remembered that Heidegger's concept of temporality is designed primarily to undercut the concept of presence-at-hand. Instead of flat images merely sitting around in consciousness, we have a dynamic tension between several elements. In my room are tables, chairs, a fireplace, couches, and so forth. But something rather dramatic is at work here. I do not create the pieces of furniture; they are given in the room from the very moment I arrive. Nor do I still have the power to create my own past history. In short, I find myself thrown into the world — yet I am not only thrown. The entities present in the room are not just obvious and boring lumps of presence, since my own reality affects how they appear to me. A child, dog, or ant would not encounter the room in the same way that I do. The things I encounter are *projected* in terms of my own possibilities, which differ from the possibilities of all other creatures. In other words, the entities in the room are torn in two separate directions. They pre-exist the situation in the room, yet also gain their meaning from their reference to my own specific potentialities. And these two moments of thrownness and projection are exactly what Heidegger means by "past" and "future." The latter have nothing to do with a real past and future, since they refer only to elements that are located entirely in the present.

To push the point further, we might imagine time frozen completely in its tracks by a witch, a wizard, or a mere thought experiment. Time now ceases to flow, and remains stranded in a single instant. Note that while Bergson might question whether such a thought experiment is even possible, there is nothing in Heidegger to prevent it. We are now left with an isolated cinematic frame of time of the most anti-Bergsonian character. Is Heidegger's theory also violated by this frozen moment of time? Not at all. His temporal analysis still works perfectly well in this case. For even in this frozen instant I still encounter the various physical masses in the room, occupy my own pre-given body, and inhabit a mind always already shaped by my personal history and that of my ancestors. And this is all that is meant by the Heideggerian past; for it is not a genuine past left behind us, but simply the givenness of all that into which we are thrown in the present moment. The same holds true for the Heideggerian future, which (as Levinas notes in *Time and the Other*) has nothing to do with a genuine future still to come, but only with what is added to the past by the one who encounters it. Even in the thought experiment of a frozen moment devoid of a literal future, I 'project' different possibilities on the same environment from what Picasso, Napoleon, Cleopatra, or a kitten would project. Even though any real past or future has vanished from the picture, past and future in the Heideggerian sense are still fully operative. I am still thrown into surroundings that are pre-given to me, and still add something of my own by interpreting them in accordance with my own potentialities. Heidegger's temporality merely alerts us to the ambiguities found in any given instant, and has nothing at all to do with time in the usual sense of the term.

Hence we should not be duped by the word "time" in the title of Heidegger's major book. Heidegger is not Bergson or Deleuze, not someone who thinks that individual states of actual things are sterile abstractions from a deeper movement of flux or becoming. Individual moments or entities are perfectly legitimate for him, as long as we remember the threefold ambiguity at work in all of them. In a sense this should already be clear from Heidegger's keen interest in the *Augenblick*, or "moment of vision." He does not mean to replace the isolated moment with a continual flux that cannot be sliced into individual points, but wants instead to replace the simplistic moment with one that is torn in three directions. When Heidegger and Bergson speak of time, they are thinking of two completely different problems. In fact, Heidegger can even be identified with the tradition of occasionalist philosophy, since he is perfectly willing to isolate instants from one another. There is no principle in his thinking that links one moment with the next, since he is only concerned with showing the surprising triple drama already underway in any individual moment.

C. The Monotony of Heidegger

Nor is this all. Many other themes in Heidegger's philosophy also collapse into the ambiguous threefold structure masquerading under the name of "time". Heidegger is not a thinker of great diversity, but is instead a figure more like Parmenides, whose greatness lies in the profoundly repetitive simplicity of his thought. Throughout Heidegger's writings we find repeated threefold structures, and these always turn out to reduce to the same triplicity just described in the case of time. A situation is given (past), but is interpreted differently according to which entity is doing the interpreting (future), and the two of these combine into a new and ambiguous model of the present. By always having recourse to this threefold structure, Heidegger's method is generally one of implosion rather than expansion, and as a result his range of topics is stunningly limited. In order to gain a better sense of this fact, we might consider just two of his failed attempts to discuss concrete realities: animal life and technology.

Heidegger's most detailed analysis of animal life is found in his famous 1929/30 Freiburg lecture course, *The Fundamental Concepts of Metaphysics*.[26] This is among the most beloved of his works, perhaps because its subject matter *feels* so especially concrete. His discussions of boredom in this book contain some of his best phenomenological descriptions: killing time at a minor provincial railway station, a splendid party that is boring nonetheless, and a desolate Sunday in the center of a European city. And his discussions of animal life provide numerous fascinating anecdotes drawn from the study of bees: they are sliced in half while feeding, or deliberately confused by researchers who move their hives during their absence. But it would be wrong to think that the concreteness of these anecdotes also entails a greater concreteness in Heidegger's subject matter. In particular, his threefold classification of human, animal, and stone in this work remains highly abstract. As Heidegger depicts it, the human has world, the stone is worldless, and the animal is "poor" in world. The poverty of the animal is a problem that he not only fails to solve, but one that he fails to elucidate altogether. In one respect, the difference between stones and humans seems clear enough to common sense. While stones are merely knocked around in the world by blind causal relations, humans see world "as" world. But even if we accept this point, Heidegger still has the problem that he uses the "as" in a twofold sense: referring both to the fact of any access to reality at all, and also as a measuring stick by which to judge certain forms of cognition as superior to others. Obviously the animal must in some crude sense encounter world "as" world, or it would be the same sort of thing as a stone. But the human is supposed to possess a higher form of the as-structure, and the philosopher an even higher form of the "as" than the average human. The problem is that in all his discussions of animal life, Heidegger gives us nothing more than a repetition of the monotonous interplay between reality on the one hand and reality "as" reality on the other. Never does he succeed in developing this rather abstract schema into a theory capable of accounting for diverse entities of various sorts.

The next issue is Heidegger's theory of technology, so unjustly praised by many observers. It would be easy to complain that Heidegger is too pessimistic about technology. But while this would be a justified critique, it would also miss the central point, since the problem would be equally severe if Heidegger were an excessive *optimist* about technology. It is less a matter of Heidegger being too harsh towards technology than of being insufficiently detailed about it. One symptom of this attitude can be found in his infamous statement that mechanized farming is metaphysically no different from the production of corpses in gas chambers, and another is his assertion that Hiroshima was not an event of such great significance, since the atom bomb actually exploded long before its actual detonation, from the ancient dawn of the forgetting of being.[27] Just as he was unable to distinguish between humans and various sorts of animals, so too is he unable to distinguish between different technological artifacts. In short, what Heidegger really gives us is not a full-blown theory of technology, but just another complaint about presence-at-hand.

Technology strips things of their mystery and turns them into a calculable stockpile of present-at-hand materials, manipulable for human purposes rather than allowed to be what they intrinsically are. In this respect his criticisms of technology are no different from his complaints about the history of philosophy, which he views as an endless parade of presence-at-hand in which one privileged entity is forever used to explain all the others.

In other words, almost all of Heidegger's philosophy collapses into a repetitive dualism between ready-to-hand and present-at-hand, or tool and broken tool. He is obsessed with the reality that withdraws from all representation and with the presence to which it is always reduced, and he expertly detects that presence at work just about everywhere in the history of philosophy and in everyday life. Indeed, the assault on presence in his works is so constant that the key technical term in all of Heidegger is perhaps not being, time, nothingness, or event, but *bloß*: the German word for "mere" or "merely." Whenever Heidegger says "mere," it is a critique of the lingering biases of presence-at-hand in any given situation. For instance, he tells us delightedly that entities are not a mere sum of realia that serve to fill up a room, and also that Hölderlin's *polla ta deina* is not a massive aggregate of uncanny on-hand entities. There will prove to be only one exception to this obsession with the alternation of presence and absence: a strange second axis in Heidegger's thinking. As will soon be described, it is this second axis that yields the mysterious fourfold found in the later years of his philosophy.

D. The Realism of Tool-Beings

The resistance to philosophical realism usually stems from a simple but tenacious point: "If we try to think a world outside human thought, then we are *thinking* it, and hence it is no longer outside thought. Any attempt to escape this circle is doomed to contradiction." This is not just a word trick: it is the tacit or explicit credo of a now lengthy tradition of philosophy that might be called the Philosophy of Human Access. Though the argument first flowered in the German Idealism of two centuries ago, it is still viewed in many quarters as the gold standard of philosophical rigor. By contrast with this remorseless and daring argument, any appeal to realism tends to sound like a stuffy, bourgeois gesture by reactionary killjoys. Consider the case of Slavoj Žižek, perhaps the most prominent representative of continental philosophy in the world today, and an emphatic proponent of the anti-realist argument just cited. In Žižek's published interviews with Glyn Daly, we find a number of radical claims to this effect. For instance: "and now I will say something horrible for which some people, especially historians of older philosophy, would lynch me — that Kant was the *first philosopher*. With his transcendental turn, I think that Kant opened up a space from which we can in retrospect read the entire canon of previous philosophy. Pre-Kantian philosophy cannot think this transcendental aspect."[28] And even more astonishingly: "The true formula of materialism is not that there is some noumenal reality beyond our distorting perception of it. The only consistent materialist position is that *the world does not exist*.... The notion of the world as a positive universe presupposes an external observer, an observer not caught in it."[29]

Žižek's landscape of possible philosophies shows stark contrasts. On one side we have pre-Kantian realism (which for him is not yet truly philosophy) with its ontology of an objective and scientific world. On the other side there is Žižek's preferred alternative, which takes Kant's transcendental turn to be a pivotal advance, denies that any "noumenal" world exists apart from some external observer, and oddly calls itself "materialism" despite its rejection of a real world. Despite my admiration for Žižek's sheer animal *gusto* as a thinker, his position as just described is the diametrical opposite of the truth. But our topic here is not Žižek, whose position is too specific to represent all the anti-realist philosophies of today's *avant garde*. Žižek is cited only to indicate that the energy and momentum of today's philosophical populace still favors the claim that we cannot think something without thinking it, thereby returning us to an inescapable closed circle of thought. Instead of agreeing with me that this position is a claustrophobic honey trap, many others celebrate it as the very condition of philosophical rigor, by contrast with the "naive realism" defended by the unreflective dupes of shallow common sense. But if I call for an escape from the closed circle of Žižek and his confederates, this is not in the name of the dusty, oppressive realism of yesteryear, but of a weird realism that shows the human-world circle to be indefensibly narrow. The remainder of this section aims to show that the Philosophy of Human Access is both inadequate and false.

We should begin by noting the obvious fact that the Philosophy of Access is completely implausible by the standards of everyday common sense. But not only is this violation of common sense not viewed as a problem: it is taken as a point of pride. Recall the famous passage from Berkeley's major work: "It is indeed an opinion strangely prevailing amongst men, that houses, mountains, rivers, and in a word all sensible objects have an existence natural or real, distinct from their being perceived by the understanding."[30] Berkeley delights in shocking the assumptions of common sense, and the same delight can be found in later figures, including Žižek himself. But of course the position is not designed only to shock: it is meant to establish a rigorous first principle on which all other philosophical knowledge should be based. Vast kingdoms filled with "houses, mountains, rivers" are remorselessly slaughtered on the altar of deduction. But the strength of this position is also its weakness: stripped of all plausibility and all extra-human scope, the legitimacy of the Philosophy of Access is based entirely on its claim to superior deductive rigor; if this supposed rigor turns out to be nonexistent, it has little else working in its favor.

The cosmos seems to be gigantic in both space and time. It is more ancient than all our ape-like ancestors and all other life forms. It might also seem safe to assume that the trillions of entities in the cosmos engage in relations and duels even when no humans observe them. However interesting we humans may be to ourselves, we are apparently in no way central to the cosmic drama, marooned as we are on an average-sized planet near a mediocre sun, and confined to a tiny portion of the history of the universe. All these apparent facts are sacrificed, in the name of superior rigor, by Kant's Copernican philosophy and its successors. It is said that all statements about distant time and space apart from humans are statements *by humans*, and hence we are trapped in the same circle as before.[31] This is a huge philosophical gamble, justified only by the desire for an unshakeable first principle on which the remainder of knowledge can be built. But before proceeding to consider the surprising *weakness* of this principle, we should note that philosophy is not geometry. In a deductive science like geometry, knowledge does in fact proceed via deduction from solid first principles. But even if we assume that those principles are rigorous in geometry (and the foundations of that discipline remain controversial) it is by no means clear that philosophy can or should follow the same method. For in the first place, a single faulty deduction in geometry invalidates entire chains of proof, while the steps of philosophical knowledge have more autonomy from their predecessors and successors: one can find grievous errors in the first principles of Plato or Aristotle yet still profit from the insights to which they lead. And in the second place, geometry only draws inferences from the nature of various points, lines, and shapes, while philosophy seeks to understand the cosmos as a whole. And its errors in grasping that cosmos arise less through faulty initial principles and false deductions than through overly abstract proclamations. When Parmenides says "being is, and non-being is not," the problem lies not in his violation of common sense, but in the utterly inadequate character of this first principle, which veers toward the useless rather than the false.

No one has seen these things more clearly than Whitehead. Early in *Process and Reality* we find a famous and stirring passage:

> It has been remarked that a system of philosophy is never refuted, it is only abandoned. The reason is that logical contradictions, except as temporary slips of the mind — plentiful, though temporary — are the most gratuitous of errors, and usually they are trivial. Thus, after criticism, systems do not exhibit mere illogicalities. They suffer from inadequacy and incoherence.[32]

Whitehead continues: "The verification of a rationalistic scheme is to be found in its general success, and not in the peculiar certainty, or initial clarity, of its first principles."[33] And finally: "Metaphysical categories are not dogmatic statements of the obvious; they are tentative formulations of the ultimate generalities."[34] When judged by the standards of Whitehead, the Philosophy of Access looks wrongheaded. Its entire claim to prestige is based on the supposed certainty and clarity of its principle that "when we think of the noumena we thereby convert them into phenomena, and hence philosophy can deal only with the phenomenal." In so doing it reduces all relations between inanimate objects to the conditions by which humans witness those relations. While philosophy is charged with knowing the whole of reality, the Philosophy of Access reduces that reality to the tiny portion of it directly available to humans. In this way it exhibits inadequacy, and thus it sows the seeds of its own eventual abandonment. Whitehead's points may not be full-blown "arguments," but they are revealing signals that something is wrong with the Philosophy of Access.

Nonetheless, I hold that the human-world circle is not even powerful as an argument. Consider our recurring example of a tree. In addition to the tree as present to us, we might also wish to speak of the tree apart from our thinking of it. "But this is impossible," the argument goes, "for in thinking of the tree as unthought, I thereby *think* it, and contradict what I was initially claiming to do." Two possible inferences can be drawn from this claim, one stronger and the other weaker. The stronger assertion is that there really is *nothing* outside the human-world coupling, as Berkeley and Žižek both hold. The weaker, more sceptical position is that we cannot *know* whether there is anything outside the human-world pair, and thus we are unable to move our thinking outside it; all thought is really just about thoughts. Now, the stronger claim is easy enough to refute, as was famously done in recent decades by the cantankerous analytic philosopher David Stove of Australia.[35] When seeking to award a prize for the worst argument in the history of philosophy, Stove settled on the absolute idealist argument, which is now known sarcastically as "Stove's Gem." For here is the problem: to say that *my thought* of the tree cannot exist without my thinking it is a mere tautology. But to conclude from this that *the tree* cannot exist without my thinking it goes beyond tautology, and of course no tautology can lead us to a non-tautologous conclusion. Indeed, this very problem is why most people prefer the weaker skeptical position to the more absolute claim that is still found with refreshing candor in the writings of Žižek.

In other words, many people will admit it is unjustified to say that "there is no being without thinking." Yet they will still retreat to the ostensibly more rigorous thesis that "there is no *thinking* without thinking." To think of a tree may not prove that there are no trees outside thought, but does prove that there are no *thoughts* about trees outside thought, and in this way philosophy still remains trapped in the circle of thinking. Against this maneuver, I hold that the phrase "there is no thinking without thinking" is not a harmless tautology. Instead, just like the absolute idealist position, it uses a tautology to make a crafty insinuation that goes beyond tautology.

This weaker Philosophy of Access claims to be more cautious than Berkeley and Žižek. Whereas these latter authors state outright that no world exists outside our confronting it, the weak version merely says: "Who knows if there really is such a world? We assert only that there is no way to *think* it, because to think it immediately turns it into an object of thought." But notice what happens as a result of this claim. The Weak Access position holds that when I refer to "the tree insofar as it is unthought," this is itself a thought. And this entails that when I say (a) "the tree insofar as it is *unthought*," what I really mean is (b) "the tree insofar as it is *thought*," since (a) is already a thought. The two statements are treated as synonymous. In short, the Weak Philosopher of Access regards the phrase "unthought tree" not just as wrong, but as *meaningless*. And thus it is that the skeptic immediately flips into an absolute idealist, since the phrase "things in themselves" is emptied of all possible meaning, and is just another way of saying "things for us." And yet there is still another way to look at the problem, for it is false to hold that "tree outside thought" means the same as "thought of a tree outside thought." In the first case I refer explicitly to the tree apart from my thinking of it; here, its qualities remain mysterious and at least partly unknown. By contrast, in the second case everything is already there for the taking: for I am speaking of the accessible *thought* of a tree, not of a tree hidden outside that thought.

If someone were to say "I cannot understand Obama," it would be absurd to reply: "You have just contradicted yourself, since you claim not to understand Obama, yet you have just spoken of him, which proves that you do understand who he is."

The situation here is the same as Meno's famous paradox:[36] (a) if you know what you are searching for, there is no need to search; (b) if you do not know what you are searching for, then it is impossible to find it; (c) therefore, searching is either pointless or impossible. This supposed paradox has been repeatedly pummeled over the years, first by Socrates and then by various logicians, as relying on an equivocation. For on the one hand to know something implies that we know it in its details, while on the other hand to know something means simply to have some sense of what it is. In other words, there is no real paradox in both knowing and not knowing Obama, since "knowing" means two different things in the two cases. The solution offered by Socrates remains the true solution: we have some grasp of the subject, but never an exhaustive one.

This fact has been familiar to students of Plato for many centuries. But the strange thing is that the Philosopher of Access makes a claim that is strikingly similar to Meno's. For according to this position: (a) you cannot think the unthought while thinking it (because then it would be a thought), and (b) you also cannot think of the unthought while not thinking of it (for obvious reasons). Therefore, (c) there can be no thinking of the unthought. But here again, "thought" means two completely different things in the two cases. To think of something is to make it present to the mind, but also to point at its reality insofar as it lies beyond its presence to the mind. A comparable point is made throughout Saul Kripke's *Naming and Necessity*,[37] one of the greatest works of analytic philosophy. For Kripke, names are "rigid designators" that point to (or stipulate) realities beyond all possible descriptions of them. For instance, we can define Christopher Columbus as "the first European to travel to America." But when this statement is later falsified by Viking archaeologists in Canada, we do not say: "In that case, Columbus is no longer Columbus." What we say instead is this: "It has been determined that Columbus actually did not discover America. Rather, the Vikings found it first." In other words, we spoke quite effectively of Columbus at the beginning even though our description of him was actually false.

The choice is not just between speaking of something or not speaking of it. We all know a way of speaking of a thing without quite speaking of it: namely, we *allude* to it. Allusion occurs in thinking no less than in speaking. To say "the tree that lies outside thinking" is neither a successful statement about a thought nor a failed statement about a thing. Instead, it is an allusion to something that might be real but which cannot become fully present. And that is why philosophy is *philosophia*: love of wisdom rather than wisdom itself. The Philosophy of Access wants philosophy to be a wisdom about thought, when really it is a *love* of wisdom about that which lies *beyond* thought. For this reason, we should rewrite Berkeley's passage as follows: "It is indeed an opinion strangely prevailing amongst modern philosophers, that houses, mountains, rivers, and in a word all sensible objects have no existence natural or real, distinct from their being perceived by the understanding."

Indirect Causation

This book has portrayed objects as existing in their own right, as autonomous from their relations with other things. But in that case it might be wondered how they interact at all, since total autonomy is incompatible with relations of any sort, and partial autonomy has yet to be explained. Given that things obviously *do* seem to interact, this might be viewed as an artificial problem: for what is the point of separating objects only to bring them back into contact again? Yet the point is that they are never brought *completely* back into contact; the reality of objects is never fully deployed in their relations. Instead of trying to eliminate the paradox of objects and relations by turning the world into nothing but a system of relations, we need to understand the polarizations at work in objects themselves.

And here we reach a point where many of the classical problems of philosophy are gathered. For along with the difference between objects and relations, we have those between objects and accidents and objects and qualities. In one sense a thing does have many different features, but in another sense it does not, since each thing is one. How is it possible for an object both to have and not to have features? Insofar as the object is a unified pole while its qualities are diverse, we encounter here the ancient problem of the one and the many, though here the "one" refers to each individual unit rather than a single cosmic lump. Furthermore, insofar as real objects have reality outside experience while sensual objects exist only within experience, we also encounter something like the mind-body problem, though I will soon suggest that this cannot be restricted to human or even animal minds. All of these problems involve polarizations between objects and one of four other terms: accidents, relations, qualities, and moments.

A. Occasionalism and Scepticism

The theme of indirect causation is not new in philosophy, but has venerable roots. It could be said that the ancient world produced two dominant models of causation: the neo-Platonism that views cause in the vertical terms of a higher world emanating into the lower, and the Aristotelian model of horizontal causation between individual substances. But a third option entered philosophy through the early Islamic theology of Iraq: occasion-alism. Certain passages of the *Qur'an* refer to important actions that may have seemed to occur naturally, but which were actually performed directly by Allah. A group of theologians in Basra, led by Abu al-Hasan al-Ash'ari, drew broad conclusions from these verses and held that nothing but Allah could affect anything else directly. These Ash'arites, as they came to be known, endorsed a divine monopoly on all relations. Created entities were depicted as islands cut off not only from each other, but even from their own accidents, which had to be supplied directly by God. And since even duration was viewed as an accident, no created object was viewed as inherently durable; each would perish in an instant if not for God continuing to grant it the accident of duration. Given this direct divine inter-vention in everything that occurred, the early occasionalists emphasized God's omnipotence to a staggering degree: he could make two plus two equal five, allow someone sitting at home in Baghdad to be simultaneously inside a tent in Mecca, and even send a good man to hell or an evil one to heaven for no reason at all. In this sense the Islamic occasionalists belonged to an "irrationalist" camp opposed by the Muslim heirs of Greece, especially Avicenna and Averroes.

There are no clear examples of occasionalism in medieval Christian philosophy. Francisco Suárez notes that when Thomas

Aquinas criticizes the occasionalist doctrine, he does not list any of its adherents by name. Nor does Suárez himself (writing in the 1590's) seem to know who they are.[38] But in fact, although Suárez opposes divine intervention in all cases short of miracles and the creation of new souls at conception, he himself draws close to one aspect of the occasionalist doctrine when he says that things do not touch directly, but only by way of their accidents (by which he means their *qualities*). Still, it is only with Descartes that Europe has its first strong taste of this formerly Islamic doctrine. The two kinds of created substance for Descartes, *res cogitans* and *res extensa*, are of different kinds and hence cannot interact directly; only God can bridge the gap between them. In this way a somewhat tedious mind-body problem was born, whereas in Islam there had been a wider and more interesting body-body problem as well. This same wider problem reappears in France when Cordemoy and Malebranche break extended substance into pieces, so that God must take part in inanimate interactions in a way not needed by the Cartesian philosophy. The term "occasionalism" is often used too restrictively to refer to those seventeenth century French philosophies in which God intervenes directly and repeatedly in every instant. But in fact the term deserves wider application to all philosophies in which things do not interact directly, but only by passing through God. In this sense the term deserves to be applied to Spinoza, Leibniz, and Berkeley, and in the past century even to Whitehead, who holds that God harbors the "eternal objects," the universal qualities by which every entity objectifies every other.[39] Such occasionalism is of obvious historical interest, but in the eyes of many it belongs only to history. In Western societies, though not in my adopted homeland of Egypt, it is now rare to meet people who see the hand of God at work in every least event, whether it be dogs fighting in the street or grains of dust falling to the ground.

But there is another philosophy of much greater prestige in our time, one that might easily be described as an inverted or upside-down occasionalism. I refer to the empirical or skeptical philosophy associated most closely with Hume. If occasionalism grants the existence of substances while denying that they can relate, empiricism performs the reverse maneuver, beginning with relations while denying that they necessarily involve independent substances. The link between impressions or ideas is not problematic for Hume; it always already exists, in the form of *habitual* links built up through customary conjunction. An apple may be nothing more than a nickname for a bundle of qualities pasted together, but human habit does in fact paste them together. What this doctrine shares with occasionalism, despite the obvious inversion, is that both grant a monopoly on relations to a single entity. Today it is easy to laugh at occasionalists who say that all relations pass through God, but no one laughs when it is said that they all pass through human experience instead. The latter might initially seem more rigorous, since we all have direct access to human experience while only a handful of mystics claim direct access to God. But the principle remains the same in both cases. Relations are denied to all entities, but in the end they are hypocritically allowed to just *one*: either the almighty God of religion, or the almighty empiricist God known as the human.

In this respect it should be clear that the occasionalist problem never really died, but was merely inverted into the positions of Hume and Kant, the two philosophers who guard acceptable mainstream philosophy from the wild borderlands of dogmatic metaphysics. In the twenty-first century one can still be a literal disciple of Hume or Kant and have a perfectly successful academic career. But outside certain religious circles, few observers would keep a straight face if you were to proclaim your literal belief in the philosophies of Avicenna, Aquinas, or even Leibniz.

B. The Point of Contact

We have seen that real objects cannot touch. Their reality consists solely in being what they are, not in some sort of impact on other things. An object is not a bundle of qualities, and for this reason a thing cannot be reproduced simply by duplicating all of its qualities and bundling them together. At most this would give us an externally convincing simulacrum of the thing, not the thing itself. This is why nothing can be modeled adequately by any form of knowledge, or by any sort of translation at all. In its primary sense an object is not used or known, but simply is what it is. No reconstruction of that object can step in for it in the cosmos. In this sense it cannot even be true that God is omniscient, since an omniscient entity would not just need to know all things, but *to be* all things. And even if he were capable of being all things, introspection is no more exhaustive than knowledge gained from the outside, and hence God cannot even fully understand *himself*. This would have serious ramifications for any attempt at an object-oriented theology, and already has profound consequences for the theory of knowledge, since it implies that no scientific model will ever succeed in replacing a thing by listing its various features. Access to the things themselves can only be indirect.

But the following objection to this theory often arises: why exaggerate and say that things cannot touch at all? Does it not seem instead that things *partly* make contact with each other? After all, we have been speaking all along of how humans have partial access to hammers while using them, and have also reflected on how fire touches certain qualities of cotton despite not touching the cotton as a whole. The problem is that objects cannot be touched "in part," because there is a sense in which objects have no parts. It is not as if things were made of seventy or eighty qualities and there were a mere practical limit ensuring that five or six of the qualities would always be withheld from the organs of sense. For even if we were to perceive every quality of an object perfectly, we would still not reconstruct the thing in its reality. To be an object means to be itself, to enact the reality in the cosmos of which that object alone is capable. It does not mean to possess X number of qualities, since these qualities serve at best as instructions for how to identify it from the outside. Objects are unified, like Leibniz's monads. There are certainly detachable parts associated with them, just as there are tiny component pieces that give rise to them. But this does not mean that the object is reducible, whether downward to its pieces or upward to its analyzable traits. Though it does seem true that we are able to make contact with certain parts (or qualities) of a hammer or cotton ball, this merely pushes the problem a step further, since it is still unclear how those parts touch the object itself.

But although we never touch real objects, we always touch sensual objects. Sensual objects would not even exist if they did not exist for me, or for some other agent that expends its energy in taking them seriously. And here we have our first case of a pair that differs from the four aforementioned tensions between objects and their qualities. What we have, in short, is a real object in *direct* contact with a sensual one. For the "I" that is sincerely absorbed in dealing with trees, wolves, or beach balls is the real me, not a sensual one. My life is truly absorbed in dealing with these objects. This contact between real and sensual objects is quite unique, replicated nowhere else on our emerging map of the world. For real objects forever withdraw from one another into the shadows of the world, and sensual objects are no better than contiguous with each other through a real object that happens to be experiencing both at the same time.

Consider the skyline of a giant city, filled with countless spires and towers. Insofar as these are all merely sensual objects, they obviously cannot make contact except through the deputy or mediator who experiences them. And insofar as they are real objects I cannot come into contact with them, for the simple reason that real objects always recede from one another. In a sense, this means that we already have a rough preliminary solution to the causal problem posed by occasionalism. If contact in the realm of the real is utterly impossible, but contact in the sensual realm is an absolute requirement, then obviously the sensual realm of experience must be where all causation is triggered. The real objects that withdraw from all contact must somehow be translated into sensual caricatures of themselves, and these exaggerated profiles are what must serve as fuel for the causal relations that are impossible between concealed real things. Somehow, the events that occur in the sensual sphere must be capable of a retroactive effect on the reality that lies outside all experience. And I will claim later that not all experience is of the human or even animal kind.

C. The Asymmetry of Contact

A few words on asymmetry are now in order. Real objects cannot touch real objects, and in this respect Heidegger's tool-analysis reawakens the occasionalist scenario. And sensual objects do not touch other sensual objects, but exist only as contiguous in a single experience that serves as their bridge. For this reason the only possible kind of direct contact is *asymmetrical*, with real objects touching the sensual objects that they experience. This contradicts the usual assumption that causal or relational contact is always symmetrical, always transitive. If a first object touches a second, then supposedly the second cannot avoid touching the first in return: for every action, there is an equal and opposite reaction; look into the abyss and it looks back into you. But that is not what happens according to the model developed in this book. Instead, there is always just one real object involved in any interaction. If I perceive the tree, it can probably perceive me in turn. But this must occur as part of a different relation, not as the reverse side of the same one.

It is obvious that this direct contact between a real object and various sensual objects works differently from the sorts of "tensions" already described between objects and qualities. In such cases we noted the paradox that the object both has and does not have its qualities. A ripe apple must somehow have the ripeness, yet it remains the same apple both before and after the ripeness is attained, meaning that the apple maintains a certain distance from its own qualities. But the situation in which a real object touches a sensual one is different: here the contact is direct. The sensual horse, diamond, or maypole is directly before me, without need of mediators to enable us to touch. By contrast, the house I observe makes no direct contact with any of its own sensual profiles, for the simple reason that it is a sensual object and has accidents only for those who experience it. The house or dog we encounter is indifferent to all the shadows and angles and moods through which it appears to us. This yields a fascinating result. For so far, we have spoken only of the inability of *real* objects to touch, and hence of their need for mediators in order to exert force on one another. But now this also seems to be true of the four object-quality tensions as well. Perhaps even these tensions need bridges in order to relate in some way.

We now have a menagerie of interactions between various sorts of objects and qualities, one that risks boring or confusing the reader. A catalog is needed to make sense of the turmoil, just as the standard model of particle physics has since the early 1970s helped to make sense of the profusion of particles and forces in nature. The only form of direct contact we know so far is between the real object that experiences the world and the various sensual objects it encounters. There they are before me: I am absorbed by their reality. Here no bridge is needed. But none of the four tensions is quite this fortunate. Each of these polarizations between an object and qualities is possibly in need of mediation as well.

Given our four basic poles of reality, six combinations between them ought to exhaust the possible permutations of the four separate terms. But we should also consider those cases of relation in which each of the poles interacts with another of its own kind. After all, the whole point of this exercise is to solve the occasionalist problem of the relation between a real object and *another* real object, and the three parallel cases must also be considered. And as for the case of two sensual objects, we know that they do not touch others of their kind, but are merely *contiguous* in the experience of some real object that serves as their bridge. As for the contact between multiple sensual qualities, I as a real object might seem to link these qualities just as I serve as the bridge between many sensual objects. But surprisingly enough, this turns out to be false. Despite the claims of empiricism, I have no direct contact with sensual qualities at all. For precisely this is the meaning of Husserl's great discovery: I never encounter black as an isolated quality, but only as the black of ink or poison, a black infused with the style of these objects. In this way sensual objects serve as the bridge between their diverse sensual qualities. But we must also remember that if I as a real object do not serve as the bridge between sensual qualities, a different real object does. For the various qualities of a hammer do not emanate only from the sensual hammer that I have in view. They also emanate from the *real* hammer that withdraws into subterranean depths beyond all access. Sensual qualities serve two masters, like moons orbiting two planets at the same time: one visible and the other invisible. An analogous situation occurs between multiple real qualities. In one sense they all inhere in the same real object. But at the same time, a multitude of real qualities also belongs to a *sensual* hammer, dog, or tree as components of its eidos. What is beginning to emerge is a cartography of ten possible permutations of the two kinds of objects and two kinds of qualities. From the basic insights of Husserl and Heidegger, a strange but refreshing geography of objects begins to emerge, leading to results that can barely be guessed. But we are getting a bit ahead of our mentors, since Heidegger never develops his own permutations of being beyond the number four.

FIGURE 4: The Ten Possible Links

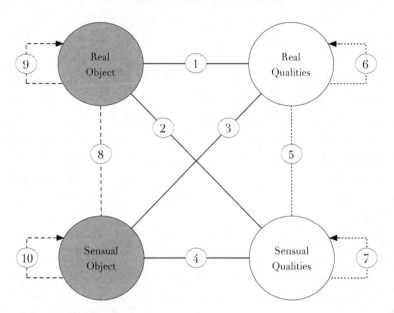

D. On Fourfold Structures

Unlike botanists, zoologists, linguists, and anthropologists, philosophers try to simplify the universe. When undertaking a census of the cosmos, they do not scavenge through countless empirical details to determine the number of basic elements at play in the world. Instead, philosophers tend to look for basic overarching structures. We are specialists in *simplicity*. But things are not altogether simple, and thus philosophy is no more master than handmaid of the other disciplines. When studying philosophers we should therefore always ask how many fundamental structures they recognize in the universe, since much of the detail of any philosophy unfolds from a small number of basic features. Not surprisingly, the numbers most commonly found in philosophy are one, two, three, and four. In those rare cases where we find larger numbers, they are generally found to be complex permutations of these simpler numerical structures.

The number one is the password of monism. Despite its comforting promise of holistic unity, it tends to be too sanguine in its implicit assertion that difference and strife are less real than a primal harmony in things. The number two seems to announce a conflict of two opposed principles. But such dualism turns out to be paradoxically monotonous, since usually nothing occurs but a constant struggle back and forth across the divide. The number three seems more sophisticated, with its claim to unify two opposed principles in a dynamic third term that both preserves and transcends the crucial features of the two opposite terms; it is essentially dualism with the introduction of a mediator, as in Hegel's dialectic and Heidegger's own repetitive threes. But the frequent danger of threefold structures is that of false happy endings that neuter the tragic force of opposition, uniting all opposites in a place too easily accessible to human resolution.

We also find a number of fourfold structures in the history of philosophy. These are always the result of two intersecting dualisms that vary greatly from one thinker to the next. Four is a powerful number in philosophy. While fully maintaining the dualist insight into the struggle of opposites, it avoids the intrinsic monotony of this struggle by spreading it onto a second axis, creating a rich tension between four poles of the world. There are many instances of such structures in intellectual history. Along with the four elements of Empedocles, Plato's divided line, and Aristotle's four causes, we find Scotus Eriugena's quadruple scheme of creation, Bacon's four idols, Kant's four groups of categories, Heidegger's *Geviert*, Greimas's semiotic square, and McLuhan's tetradic laws of media. As already noted, none of these groupings of four key terms is deduced from empirical observation of the world; instead, each emerges from the intersection of two distinct axes of division.

This procedure of laying two binary oppositions crosswise over the world is not automatically either successful or unsuccessful. The degree of success depends primarily on two criteria. Criterion number one: how well chosen are the two axes of division? To take the extreme case, it is rather easy to produce stupid versions of fourfold structures whenever we wish. If I say that everything in the world comes either from Italy or elsewhere, and is either electrically powered or not, then we have a miraculous "fourfold" philosophy in which non-Italian, non-electrical entities make up the greatest portion of the universe. But this would be ridiculous. Criterion number two: does a given fourfold system provide a useful account of how the four poles interrelate? A fourfold structure that splits the universe into four parts while leaving them in static co-existence is merely a dull taxonomy that gives little instruction as to how the universe works.

These same criteria may be used to judge the emerging fourfold structure in this book. First, how well chosen are the axes of division that we have endorsed? It seems to me that the two dualities in question are not just feasible, but inevitable to the point of being exclusive. Heidegger makes an excellent case for his tool-analysis, which gives us an axis splitting the visible profiles of things from the obscurest depths of their being. And Husserl makes a decisive point on the difference between unified sensual objects and their shifting adumbrations. We do not encounter loose pixels of quality and compress them into sloppy united bulks through the mere force of habit. Instead, we face a landscape of unified sensual objects that emanate or radiate different qualities at different times.

Once these two dualities are accepted, it immediately follows that the world is composed of four poles. These poles do not stand side-by-side in static isolation; we can already see them in tension with one another. They enter into various permutations, two at a time, and we have seen that there are ten possible combinations of terms. But the most interesting of these are the heterogeneous pairings of one object-term with one quality-term. There are four of these: four basic polarizations in the world. The reason for laying such stress on these issues is because the metaphysics developed in this book will probably seem strange, and whatever is strange often seems arbitrary or forced. But if the reader can grasp why the two axes of division are apparently so inevitable, perhaps it will be clear why the metaphysics that explores the workings of the fourfold is inevitable as well.

6

Heidegger's Fourfold

We now come to *das Geviert*, "the fourfold." It is the most notorious concept in Heidegger's writings but also one of the most neglected. When speaking of the fourfold of earth, sky, gods, and mortals, and speaking of their relations in terms of mirror-plays, weddings, dances, and songs, Heidegger seems to reach his nadir of bombastic preciousness. Few clues are given in his writings for interpreting this poetic terminology in a more rigorous theoretical framework. Most scholars have simply ignored the concept, perhaps simply out of embarrassment. A few others have confined themselves to the mere paraphrase of Heidegger's own words on the topic. Only a handful of specialists have dared to take the concept seriously, even though it saturates all of his later writings.

The topic of the fourfold first appears openly in Heidegger's lecture cycle "Einblick in das was ist"[40] ("Insight Into What Is"), delivered in December 1949 in the northern city of Bremen. As is well known, Heidegger was banned from university teaching following the war. This expulsion from academia, along with a general nervous collapse, kept him out of public view from the war's end until his appearance in Bremen, which thus marks the first work of the later phase of his career. But the 1949 lectures count as Heidegger's first late work for more than biographical reasons. An examination of his writings of the 1950's on language, technology, and "the thing" shows them to be simple developments of what was already presented in Bremen. And even a cursory reading of these 1949 lectures shows that the fourfold lies absolutely at their center. It is my view that earth, sky, gods, and mortals are not the mere poetic distractions of an elderly sage, but are instead the ultimate destination of his lengthy path of thinking.

A. The Fourfold in Heidegger

None of Heidegger's basic concepts has been more ridiculed than the fourfold. On December 1, 1949, Heidegger lectured before the Bremen Club, with its non-academic audience of shippers and industrialists. They were treated to Heidegger's first public philosophical statement since the war: "Insight Into What Is," surely the strangest masterpiece of twentieth century philosophy. The central concept of these lectures is clearly the fourfold. Six decades later, the quartet of earth, sky, gods, and mortals is still rarely discussed, let alone fully understood. The problem with downplaying the fourfold is its rather obtrusive status as the dominant concept in Heidegger's later writings, and indeed as the very root of his meditations on both language and technology. Among recent scholars it is perhaps only in the work of Jean-François Mattéi[41] that we find genuine seriousness about the crucial role of the fourfold in Heidegger's thinking. What still remains missing from Heidegger studies is an original philosophical interpretation of this concept. But in any case, 1949 in Bremen is where *das Geviert* appears in full-blown form. Here it takes the form of a poetic-sounding fourfold of earth, sky, gods, and mortals. The inherent poetry of these four terms, and the fact that Heidegger gives no clear explanation of their meaning, has led to widespread avoidance of the subject. Some interpreters hold that "four" is merely poetic slang for "many," so that any plural number would have worked equally well. Others hold that the number four is nothing more than a quaint tribute to Hölderlin, despite the fact that the four terms never appear together in any known passage of Hölderlin.

Here I will cite from the essay "The Thing," one of the better-known spinoff works from the Bremen lecture. Speaking of wine pouring from a jug, Heidegger tells us that "in thinging, [the jug] stays earth and sky, divinities and mortals."[42] These four terms are most clearly defined in another spinoff essay of the Bremen lectures, "Building Dwelling Thinking." Speaking of earth: "Earth is the serving bearer, blossoming and fruiting, spreading out in rock and water, rising up into plant and animal."[43] As for sky: "The sky is the vaulting path of the sun, the course of the changing moon, the wandering glitter of the stars, the year's seasons and their changes, the light and dusk of day, the gloom and glow of night, the clemency and inclemency of the weather, the drifting clouds and blue depth of the ether."[44] We now come to gods, who are "the beckoning messengers of the godhead. Out of the holy sway of the godhead, the god appears in his presence or withdraws into his concealment."[45] And finally, mortals: "The mortals are the human beings. They are called mortals because they can die. To die means to be capable of death *as* death."[46] This is obviously not the sort of thing that would pass for rigor in Anglo-American analytic philosophy circles.

To each of these four terms, Heidegger appends the remark that to think one of them is to think the other three as well. In "The Thing" we find further discussion of this point: "Each of the four mirrors in its own way the presence of the others. Each therewith reflects itself in its own way into its own, within the simpleness of the four. And further: "This mirroring does not portray a likeness. The mirroring, lightening each of the four, appropriates their own presencing into simple belonging to one another."[47] We not only have four poles of the fourfold. We also find that they are not isolated from one another but reflect each other, each in its own way.

Before dismissing this fourfold as a self-indulgent or even crackpot concept, we need to remember how central it is for Heidegger. As already noted, the 1949 Bremen lectures are the key to all of his later writings. Along with "The Thing" and "Building Dwelling Thinking," another Bremen spinoff is the celebrated "The Question Concerning Technology." And finally, all of Heidegger's later meditations on language are saturated with the fourfold: language is the interplay of thing and world, and this turns out to have a fourfold structure.[48] There can be no question that Heidegger is deeply serious about the fourfold.

B. Interpreting Heidegger's Fourfold

Moreover, *das Geviert* is not even especially difficult to interpret, as long as we keep a few basic principles in mind. The first of these, which ought to be obvious but is often ignored, is that the fourfold cannot refer to four specific *kinds* of objects. "Earth" does not mean strawberries and hay; "sky" does not mean comets and moons; "gods" does not signify Aphrodite, Jupiter, and Loki; and finally, "mortals" does not mean individual people such as Picasso and Virginia Woolf. The whole of Heidegger's philosophy can be read as a critique of ontotheology: the sort of traditional philosophy which holds that one *type* of entity can explain all the others — whether it be atoms, perfect forms, the *apeiron*, mental images, or power. He insists that being is deeper than any of these manifestations. Obviously, Heidegger did not suddenly abandon this critique of ontotheology from 1949 onward in order to endorse a taxonomy of the four most important kinds of beings. If Heidegger had meant to do so, we would have seen some justification for why there are four key types of entities, and why these four and no other. In the absence of such an explicit reversal, it is safe to assume that his fourfold structure is an outgrowth of his previous thinking. Further evidence for this can be gathered from the "mirroring" he describes between all four members of the fourfold, which also suggests a ubiquitous ontological structure rather than a taxonomy of four different types of entities. In short, the four terms in the fourfold cannot be taken literally to mean: (a) things down on the ground, (b) things up high in the sky, (c) deities, and (d) people. There is only one case where Heidegger seems to veer slightly from this tacit principle: in his treatment of mortals, which at times he does seem to identify literally with human entities.

Given this initial warning, it is surprisingly easy to interpret the meaning of Heidegger's fourfold. For if there is one axiom of his thinking that never varies, it is the constant opposition he draws between absence and presence, veiled and unveiled. And his choice of wording in Bremen makes it perfectly clear that earth and gods are both terms of concealment. As early as the artwork essay in 1935,[49] the task of earth is to withdraw from all access, and the same holds true in 1949. As for gods, they are said only to "hint" rather than revealing themselves. By contrast, Heidegger tells us that mortals are linked with the as-structure of explicit visibility. And as for sky, it is clearly a matter of specifically visible entities, as opposed to the ceaseless withdrawal of earth.

So much for the first Heideggerian axis, a division repetitive and profound enough that it would make Parmenides proud. But there is also a second axis in Heidegger's thinking that makes it easy to read the fourfold in a second direction as well. In 1949, that axis is a second version of the famous ontological difference, or the difference between being and beings. For there are two possible ways to read this difference. One is to read it as a distinction between veiled and unveiled, absent and present, withdrawn and cleared, implicit and explicit. But it can also be read in a second sense as meaning that being is one and beings are many. And for Heidegger, this second axis repeats itself on both levels: veiled and unveiled. For on the concealed level "earth" is always read as a single, unified force. And the same is even more obviously true on the visible level of "mortals," who are mortals not by experiencing many different things, but by encountering beings *as a whole*: namely, in the form of death "as" death. The opposite is true of the other terms. On the concealed level Heidegger says "gods" rather than God, not as some gratuitous slap at monotheism, but to show the contrast between the singular earth that withdraws and the plurality of cryptic messages that the moment of "gods" represents. And on the revealed level, the menagerie of items included under "sky" contrasts with the singularity found in earth and mortals. In other words, the fourfold can be viewed as the intersection of two related but variant senses of the ontological difference: veiled vs. unveiled, and one vs. many.

C. From Objects to World

Heidegger gave his first Freiburg Lecture Course in 1919, during the so-called War Emergency Semester. Though the philosopher was not yet thirty years old, this early lecture course is already a minor masterpiece. In the first place it already contains a full-blown version of the tool-analysis, refuting in advance the occasional strange claims that Heidegger stole this analysis from Husserl's work of the early 1920's. And beyond this, we are surprised to find that a version of the fourfold even exists already in Heidegger's 1919 course, though it differs from the full-blown later model in a crucial respect. We have seen that the fourfold of 1949 crossbreeds the distinction of veiled and unveiled with one between unity and plurality. And by unity he means the unity of the world as a whole, not of individual things. By contrast, Heidegger's second axis in 1919 more closely approaches Husserl's distinction between the unified intentional object and its plurality of traits, and I for one find it superior. Here there is still no talk of a single unified earth from which all things emerge, or a single experience of being as a whole in the Angst of mortals. The second axis in 1949 distinguishes between "beings as a whole" and individual beings such as dogs or apples. But in 1919 the distinction is the more Husserlian one between an individual apple and its plurality of traits. In short, there is a genuine sense in which Heidegger's 1949 fourfold marks a step backward from the 1919 model. To show this, we might consider several possible approaches to the sensual realm.

- Hume: there are only apple-qualities, bundled together in a unit by human habit.

- Husserl: there is a duel between the apple-object and the shifting apple-qualities on its surface.

- Heidegger (1919): there is a duel between the apple as "something at all" and its specific apple-qualities. Yet there is nothing especially applesque about its "something at all" pole. Everything is "something at all" in the same sense as everything else. This makes the "something at all" disturbingly close to Hume's "bundle," which does not differ qua bundle in our respective experiences of cotton, dogs, melons, or trees.

- Heidegger (1949): there is a duel between reality as a whole and apple-qualities. What opposes the apple-qualities is neither a bundle, nor a sensual object, nor a "something at all." Rather, they are opposed by being as a whole, which is revealed to Dasein in the experience of Angst.

In other words, the 1919 Heidegger saw a drama underway in the heart of individual entities, even if less vividly than Husserl did. But the 1949 Heidegger sees it as a drama between being as a whole and specific beings. In this way the object-oriented spirit of Heidegger's *Geviert* is compromised, and hence we must not follow him down this path. For in fact, the 1949 version of the fourfold is philosophically less sophisticated than the model of 1919.

Of the four models of the sensual realm just listed, the best is that of Husserl, whose unfortunate idealism does not contam-

FIGURE 5: Heidegger's Early Fourfold (1919)

FIGURE 6: Heidegger's Late Fourfold (1949)

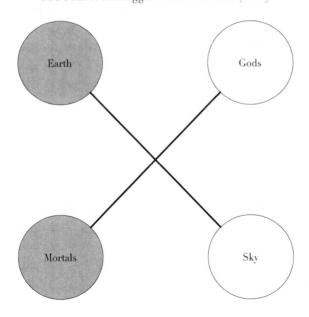

inate his remarkable insights into the intentional realm. And if we speak purely of that realm, then the worst of the four models is that of Heidegger in 1949. By establishing a counterpoint between the world as a whole and the specific entities that populate it, the Heidegger of Bremen weakens all sense of drama within specific entities. Second place in the "worst model of objects" contest for our list of four is probably a tie between Hume and the Heidegger of 1919, both of whom see a need to bind together a multitude of traits, though both do this with a kind of *vis dormitiva*: qualities are bundled together by a bundling faculty. In Hume's case *habit* is given the credit for creating the bundle, though no more explanation is given of such habit than of the workings of the occasionalist God. In the young Heidegger's case the bundle arises from the fact that each entity is "something at all," though again no explanation is offered of why certain specific qualities should be assigned to one "something at all" rather than another. But in Husserl's case we have a truly marvelous insight, in which the unity of a melon is a melon-unity quite different from a cat-unity or coin-unity. The object is a vague yet compelling integer, a somewhat durable unit encrusted with shifting exteriors. In this sense, Heidegger fails to live up to his teacher's matchless insights into the sensual realm.

But if we look beyond the sensual realm, then the picture is rather different. Here, last place on the list of four must go to Hume, with his fruitless agnosticism about what lies beyond the bounds of sensual experience. Second-to-last goes to Husserl, with his undeniable idealism that bans all reality that is not, in principle, accessible to intentionality. He edges Hume on the list for the sole but important reason that he allows sensual objects to have a *real* eidos: genuine qualities that make the sensual objects what they are, in contrast with the accidental traits swirling along their crust at any given moment. In deciding whether to give first place to the 1919 or 1949 Heidegger, we find that at both age thirty and age sixty the philosopher had an outstanding sense of the reality that withdraws from all presence to view. But as a tiebreaker, we award the trophy to the younger version of Heidegger insofar as he allows for a strife in the depths between individual objects and their qualities, and not just between reality-as-a-whole and qualities. His appeal to "earth" from 1935 onward, so often celebrated as a sensitive holistic breakthrough, is in fact a terrible relapse from his 1919 object-oriented model of phenomenology towards a half-cooked form of monism. In a sense, then, the fourfold model endorsed in this book follows Husserl when it comes to sensual objects, and the young Heidegger when it comes to real ones. While Heidegger gains in poetic force in 1949, he slips a notch as a philosopher of objects. While appeals to the supposed "world as a whole" always have an automatic air of intellectual gravitas and philosophical depth, there is no good reason to think that such an encompassing whole even exists. Instead, everything comes back to the strife between individual objects and their accidents, qualities, relations, and moments.

D. Other Problems with Heidegger's Fourfold

Throughout this book I have expressed admiration for Heidegger for choosing two effective axes for his fourfold, especially in its abandoned and underdeveloped 1919 version. But along with the question of whether the fourfold structure is built of the right two axes, we should also ask whether it gives a sufficient account of how the four poles interact. After all, given that we are talking about a fourfold structure *within* objects rather than four separate kinds of them, the four terms must be unified in the life of every object, and must therefore be related in some manner. On this point Heidegger is less helpful. Yes, he tells us that his four poles are not static but interact with one another in dramatic fashion. But he sheds little light on the mechanisms of this drama. When discussing how the four terms interact, Heidegger often provides nothing but the negative claim that they are not static. On those occasions when he does attempt to clarify their interrelations, he limits himself to poetic allusions to mirrors, weddings, dances, and songs. The image of the "mirror-play" is especially recurrent in Heidegger, though he never clarifies exactly how one term might be reflected in another. And not only that: he never even specifies whether every one of the four terms is able to mirror every other. In those cases where his diagrams of the fourfold include lines that join various pairs of terms, such diagrams usually give us nothing more than an X that links the corners diagonally. Only rarely does he draw horizontal and vertical lines as well to create a full set of six permutations. Thus, the question is never even posed. My point in saying these things is not to criticize Heidegger for his vagueness; no one expects a pioneer to establish a civilization refined to the point of decadence. My point is that we should expect *ourselves* to develop the matter a bit further than Heidegger did himself. "One requiteth a teacher badly if one remain only a scholar."[50]

There is still another problem with the fourfold. Although Heidegger already does a good job of avoiding a taxonomy of entities, he relapses slightly in at least two ways. One is by sometimes treating the pole of "mortals" as though it referred literally to *people*. The other is by restricting his examples of the fourfold to such poignant, romantic cases as Greek temples and peasant shoes. When speaking of technological artifacts such as nuclear power plants, hydroelectric dams, and mechanized farms, he seems less willing to grant any sort of dignity to these things. In fact, given that the poles of the fourfold do not exist in static isolation but only in interaction, the four terms we have described are less important than the possible fission and fusion between them, just as the four elements of Empedocles would have remained frozen without the workings of love and hate. More concretely, instead of speaking of earth, sky, gods, and mortals, it is the duel or tension between earth and sky, or gods and mortals, or any other combination of those terms, that ought to be the focus of any ontology of the fourfold object. And that is indeed the case for the position developed in this book. The model it proposes does not treat the two kinds of objects and two kinds of qualities independently, but sees them as always in tension between one object-pole and one quality-pole. We have also seen that different relations exist besides tensions between object and quality. In fact, we have seen that there are ten possible permutations in all. These must be classified and recorded, and pushed to yield results that are fruitful rather than merely pedantic.

We are now far from the beaten path of recent philosophy– far enough that the reader may need reassurance that this is not one of those homespun private ontologies easily found in the attics and basements of the internet. It is helpful to remember that despite the apparent strangeness of this fourfold model, it has powerful ancestors whose insights deserve to be honored. The quadruple structure combines the key insights of Heidegger and Husserl, both of them found on almost any short list of the great philosophers of the past century. But the metaphysics of objects has even deeper roots than this. For in a sense, this book seeks only to provide a weirder version of Aristotle's theory of substance. Heidegger's fourfold has certain features that make it fairly compelling. But when viewed closely, it fails to provide answers to a number of basic questions. For this reason, our goal should be to advance in such a way as to make it look primitive. Allow me to explain...

The highest compliment we can pay to thinkers is to grasp the central ideas of their respective systems and try to push them further. When this succeeds, it will always tend to make our predecessors look somewhat primitive — though by primitive I mean "classic" rather than "crude." We will find that they have stopped at a point where we ourselves no longer have the luxury of stopping. Our own contributions will need to display more flexibility, nuance, and scope than the originality of our predecessor. In the present day, Heidegger's fourfold structure appears to be merely a quirky and arbitrary outgrowth of his late system. But imagine a scenario in which, two centuries from now, all ontologies are built out of fourfold structures descended from his own. If that were to happen, then the status of the 1949 Bremen lectures would shift from "isolated and inexplicable oddity" to "classic ancestral text of quadruple ontology." The greatest compliment we can pay to our ancestors is not to imitate their words and gestures endlessly, but to turn them into the forerunners of something different.

7

The New Fourfold

The obvious danger of a fourfold structure is that it might seem crankish or bizarre, like a New Age doctrine or the creed of a false prophet. *Das Geviert* might lead one to imagine the leader of a cult on some remote Pacific island, with a reformed harlot on one arm and a child bride on the other, all united in worship of the Great Obsidian Cylinder where the four forces of the cosmos are stationed. Yet in the preceding chapters I have tried to show that reflection on the fourfold is inevitable once we acknowledge both the results of Heidegger's potent tool-analysis and Husserl's breakthrough into the duel between a unified sensual object and its multitude of profiles.

Our quadruple enigma arises from the strange autonomy and lack of autonomy of real and sensual objects with respect to their real and sensual traits. In this sense our problem has a highly classical flavor: the Platonic or Kantian doctrine of a world beyond the senses is fused with an Aristotelian-sounding distinction between the unity of a substance and its plurality of traits. We began with the occasionalist deadlock in which no two objects are able to make contact. Yet this turned out to be just one piece of a larger puzzle in which it is still unclear how an object makes contact even with its own qualities. While it is a serious problem to know how fire touches cotton or human touches world, it is just as hard to know how an apple relates to its own features such as cold, red, hard, sweet, tangy, cheap, and juicy in the first place. In the present chapter I will try to make this model a bit more concrete.

A. Reviewing the Four Poles

We should begin by reviewing briefly the model of Heidegger's fourfold and comparing it with the similar quadruple structure of objects as endorsed by this book. It was noted that every rigorous fourfold structure in the history of philosophy results from the crossing of a pair of dualisms. In Heidegger's case one of those dualities is perfectly clear, since it saturates the whole of his career: the monotonous interplay of shadow and light, veiling and unveiling, concealing and revealing. This challenge to philosophies of presence, this insistence on an obscure subterranean depth that haunts all accessible entities, remains the obvious core of his philosophical journey. But Heidegger's second axis of reality is a bit hazier, and shifts during various portions of his career. In 1919, it is the difference between "something at all" and "something specific," a duality placed in the heart of every entity that exists, whether present or absent for conscious view. The broken hammer is both a specific visible entity and also an entity in general, but the same holds for the hammer-being unleashed in a depth that hides from every gaze. We have seen that in 1949 the fourfold no longer plays out in the heart of every entity. Instead it involves a duel, repeated in the two arenas of the veiled and unveiled, between what Heidegger calls "beings as a whole" and "beings as such" —[51] between the world in its totality and the various specific things that populate the concealed and revealed worlds. The terms that merely hint while withdrawing from view are earth and gods; those to which we have access "as" what they are receive the names of mortals and sky. The terms that refer to the unity of the world are earth and mortals, while those that are shattered in advance into a multitude of realities are gods and sky. These four terms cannot be taken literally as a taxonomy of entities, but are four structures of reality in general, found everywhere and at all times — despite Heidegger's romantic tendency to find the quadruple mirroring structure in rustic handiwork while withholding fourfold status from despicable plastic cups and offshore oil rigs.

The version of the fourfold defended in this book is similar to Heidegger's 1919 model, but shifted in the direction of Husserl's model of intentional or sensual objects. When the young Heidegger says that every entity is both "something at all" and "something specific," the diversity of things is found only in the second of these moments. A hammer, monkey, chimney, watermelon, and star are all "specific" in different ways, but all are "something at all" in exactly the same fashion for Heidegger. In fact, to be "something at all" is a rather boring and formalistic honor that makes one entity interchangeable with the rest, despite Heidegger's occasional nods to Aristotle's principle that being is expressed in many ways. But in the case of Husserl we have seen that this does not happen, and it is Husserl's model that I wish to endorse. For if we consider the phenomenon of a watermelon in the mind, we do not find a dull opposition between (a) the melon in all its particularity, and (b) some "being in general" that would belong equally to the melon and to all other things. This is too reminiscent of Hume's bundles of qualities, with the sole difference that "being" is now adopted to serve the role of Hume's unifying bundle. Instead, the duel in question is between the watermelon as an enduring unit and the multitude of profiles that it exhibits at various times. The distinction is not between "something in general" and "specific watermelon" (as the young Heidegger would have it) but between watermelon-object and watermelon-qualities. So far Husserl is right, and should be opposed only in his idealistic claim that this watermelon-object in consciousness is not shadowed by a veiled melon-object inaccessible to every view.

The four poles of the fourfold endorsed by the present book have less poetic names than Heidegger's own. Instead of earth, gods, mortals, and sky, we offer real objects, real qualities, sensual objects, and sensual qualities. The relative lack of poetry in this newest model compared with Heidegger's is due not to some hideous aesthetic preference for desert landscapes: rather, it is because the drama for us lies not in the poles themselves, but in the tensions between them. Heidegger does refer to a dynamic interrelation of mirroring between the four terms of the fourfold, but never gives names to these tensions or considers them one by one.

The tension between sensual objects and their sensual qualities is the major topic of Husserl's phenomenology. The simplest mailbox or tree remains the same unit for us over a certain period of time, despite the radiation of ever new profiles from its surface. Though the deadening habits of common sense strip this event of its mystery, there is something permanently strange about the manner in which an enduring sensual object can appear in countless incarnations depending on the viewer's angle, distance, and mood. Perhaps children still appreciate this strangeness; in adults, strenuous exercises may be needed to recapture the atmosphere of mystery that ought to surround the merest rotation of a wine bottle or the shifting of light behind a mountain. Husserl also offers us a second tension in which the sensual object differs not from its shifting accidental facades, but from the plurality of qualities that it truly needs to remain what it is from moment to moment. But these are its real qualities, since they cannot be stripped from the sensual object without destroying it, and since they are withdrawn from all sensual access, limited to oblique approaches by the intellect. There is a further tension between real objects and their sensual qualities, as found in Heidegger's tool-analysis. The withdrawn or subterranean hammer is a concealed unit, but one that emits sensual qualities into the phenomenal sphere. And finally, these withdrawn real objects are not just unified lumps, but differ from one another insofar as each has its own essential features. The tension between the real thing as a unified thing and its multitude of qualities or notes is not discussed by Husserl or

Heidegger, but can be found in the *Monadology* of Leibniz,[52] and in the lesser-known works of the twentieth-century Basque Spaniard Xavier Zubíri.[53] Without adopting the Hölderlinian pathos of Heidegger's own terminology, we will still give these four tensions the suggestive names they deserve: *time* (SO-SQ) as in Husserl's adumbrations, *space* (RO-SQ) as in Heidegger's tool-analysis, *essence* (RO-RQ) as in Leibniz's monads, and *eidos* (SO-RQ) as in Husserl's eidetic intuition. Here at last is a fourfold structure that can serve as bedrock for further constructions.

B. Time, Space, Essence, and Eidos

Every thoughtful person occasionally reflects on the nature of time and space, which form the permanent homeland of human action and of everything else. Is time reversible, and can we travel backward and forward through it? Does space have only the three dimensions that we see, or does it contain many more, some of them populated by other life forms? Are time and space absolute and empty containers as they are for Newton, or generated by way of relations as they are for Leibniz? Is it possible to consider time and space as a single four-dimensional space-time, as Minkowski famously asserts? Such questions hold an endless fascination for us. But in all of these cases it is simply assumed that space and time are peerless continua without friend or rival. Kant, for instance, sets them apart and alone in the Transcendental Aesthetic, consigning everything else to the table of categories. But instead of taking the primal status of space and time for granted, it might be asked if both are perhaps derivative of a more basic reality. And if the answer turns out to be yes, then we should also ask whether this more primal dimension might have other offspring than its two most famous children, space and time. For this reason it must count as a dramatic development that the metaphysics of objects sketched in this book provides a rare opportunity to reinterpret

space and time in terms of something even more basic: the polarization between objects and their qualities.

When we speak of time in the everyday sense, what we are
referring to is a remarkable interplay of stability and change. In
time, the objects of sense do not seem motionless and fixed, but
are displayed as encrusted with shifting features. Nonetheless,
experience does not decay in each instant into an untethered
kaleidoscope of discontinuous sensations; instead, there seem to
be sensual objects of greater or lesser durability. Time is the
name for this tension between sensual objects and their sensual
qualities. When we speak instead of space, everyone will recall
the old quarrel between Leibniz and Clarke[54] over whether
space is an absolute container or simply a matter of relations
between things. But in fact it is neither: for space is not just the
site of relation, but rather of relation *and* non-relation. Sitting at
the moment in Cairo, I am not entirely without relation to the
Japanese city of Osaka, since in principle I could travel there on
any given day. But this relation can never be total, since I do not
currently touch the city, and even when I travel to stand in the
exact center of Osaka I will not exhaust its reality. Whatever
sensual profile the city displays to me, even if from close range,
this profile will differ from the real Osaka that forever
withdraws into the shadows of being. This interplay of relation
and non-relation is precisely what we mean when we speak of
space, and in this respect Heidegger's tool-analysis is actually
about space, not about time as he wrongly contends. Space is the
tension between concealed real objects and the sensual qualities
associated with them.

We now leave time and space and meet with their two
neglected sisters, still nameless for the moment. Husserl showed
that the sensual realm contains not only a tension between
objects and their accidental surface-qualities (which we have
now called "time"). For along with this there is another tension
between objects and their truly crucial qualities, which are

revealed through a process of eidetic variation: we imagine a house from many different viewpoints, stripping away its shifting properties that arise and then vanish. The goal of this method is to approach an inner nucleus of the house, an eidos that makes it what it is for those who perceive it. Husserl is quite clear that these eidetic features can in no way be sensual, insofar as no sense experience can possibly grasp them. Instead, they can only be known through categorial intuition: the work of the intellect and not of the senses. Such intuition points at those vital and never-visible traits that differ from the purely sensual character of the object. And this entails an articulation into parts that is foreign to the sensual object's unity. Here we find Husserl's true kinship with Plato. As opposed to the philosophies of individual substance that place qualities on the surface of the world and view the object as a hidden substratum in the depths, both Plato and Husserl reverse this assumption: putting a multitude of eidetic qualities in the depths while the object unifies them on the surface of the world. This tension between sensual objects and their real hidden qualities is what Husserl calls the *eidos*. And finally there is the fourth and final tension, never accessible to human experience. I refer to the duel, underway in hidden real things, between the unified real object and its multitude of real hidden features. This tension between the real object and its real qualities has always been called its *essence*, though traditional realism lacks Heidegger's remorseless sense that the real is entirely withdrawn from all access. And as a reminder, whereas the traditional model of essence treated real qualities as mobile universals able to be exemplified anywhere, qualities according to the present book are shaped by the object to which they belong, just as the moons of Jupiter are molded by their planetary lord.

In this way the monotonous age-old coupling of time and space is expanded into a new model encompassing four tensions between objects and their qualities: time, space, essence, and eidos. These four terms can be stated in any order; this one is preferred merely because it has the most melodious ring in my ears. We have already determined that the world is apportioned into exactly two kinds of object and two kinds of quality. Their possible pairings lead to precisely these four tensions and no others. The interaction of time, space, essence, and eidos is not the play of four disembodied forces, but of four tensions affecting every object that in some way is. Note that these tensions already encompass both real and fictitious entities, given that sensual objects join real ones as a basic feature of the model. Reductionist, science-worshipping naturalism can never accomplish or even appreciate this feat, since it is in too great a hurry to exterminate all the millions of entities that do not flatter its crude bias in favor of physical things.

C. On Fission and Fusion

Although tensions are always interesting, they sometimes still lead nowhere. The opposed armies of Korea have stared each other down for over fifty years with only minor incidents, and may well do so for another century or more. The same is true of the tensions between the various forms of objects and qualities. In order for something to change in the *status quo*, the bond between object and quality must be dissolved and a new one produced. To use a metaphor from applied physics, we need fission accompanied by fusion. But fission and fusion are the only two options, and they must always go hand in hand, since objects and qualities never exist outside of some bond that must be ruptured if another is to emerge. Now, we have just finished naming our four kinds of tension: time, space, essence, and eidos. It will be worthwhile to give a quick preview of what it means when each of these tensions is ruptured or produced.

Time was described as the strife between a sensual object and its numerous sparkling features. Dogs and trees display an excess of carnal detail that shifts in each moment without our viewing them as different objects. This is the very nature of perception, and I will soon claim that primitive perception is found even in the nethermost regions of apparently mindless entities. But of course we do not remain focused forever on a steady landscape of enduring sensual objects; rather, there are intermittent changes in what we confront. This can happen in at least two ways. Perhaps we identify something differently all of a sudden: we find that the tree was in fact a gallows, so that its surface qualities now shift into a far more sinister key. Or perhaps we shift our attention from a sensual object to its neighbors: from a strawberry to its seeds, or perhaps to the strawberry patch as a whole. When this happens there is a momentary breakdown in the former balance between sensual objects and their qualities; the object is briefly exposed as a unified kernel dangling its qualities like marionettes. This event could be called recognition or acknowledgment, but these terms suggest an intricate cognitive process that should perhaps be restricted to more advanced animal entities. What we really need is a term applicable to the primitive psyches of rocks and electrons as well as to humans. I propose the term *confrontation* as sufficiently broad for the task. Wakeful humans confront strawberries and commando raids, a sleeper confronts the bed, and a pebble confronts the asphalt that it strikes as opposed to all the accidental details of that asphalt.

Space was described as the tension between real objects that lie beyond access, and their sensual qualities which exist only when encountered. Whereas sensual objects are conjoined with their qualities in advance, such that fission between the poles is required, the real object is absent from the sensual field; hence, real object and sensual qualities will meet only when *fused*. In such cases the sensual qualities are stripped from their current sensual overlord and appear to orbit a withdrawn *real* object, an invisible sun bending them to its will. The very invisibility of the object makes it impossible to compress the object together with its sensual qualities into a bland purée, as often happens in boring everyday experience. This fusion occurs for example in artworks of every sort, and I would suggest further that Heidegger's "broken tools" also have an aesthetic effect, if not a strictly artistic one. Instead of the direct sort of contact that we have with sensual objects, there is an allusion to the silent object in the depths that becomes vaguely fused with its legion of sensual qualities. As a general term for the fusion of withdrawn real objects with accessible surface qualities, we can use the word *allure*. As I define the term in my book *Guerrilla Metaphysics*,[55] "allure is a special and intermittent experience in which the intimate bond between a thing's unity and its plurality of [specific qualities] somehow partially disintegrates."

In Husserl's case we noticed that sensual objects not only have accidental surface profiles. They also have an eidos, or qualities crucial for the object to be acknowledged as what it is. These qualities do not press against us like sensual ones. Grasped only by categorial and not sensuous intuition, they are never fully present. The sensual object has a vague and unified effect on us, not usually articulated into its various eidetic features. It is always fused in advance with its own eidos. Only theoretical labor can disassemble or reverse-engineer the bond between them. The word *theory* can serve as our term for the fission that splits a unified sensual object from the real qualities it needs in order to be what it is. We will have to decide later whether animals, plants, and airplanes are also capable of theory in some primitive sense. But for now, we can already see that theory is a kind of fission between a sensual object and its multitude of real traits.

Finally, we spoke of essence as the tension between a real object and its real qualities. This relation never enters directly into any experience, since both of its poles are withdrawn from all access. Leibniz was correct in noting the following paradox: to be is to be one, since a real object must be unified; however, a mere unit would be interchangeable with any other, and thus no two monads would be different. Thus, each real object must have a *multitude* of real traits. I will now suggest is something strange: namely, the object itself does not have its own essential features. We saw already that the real object has no contact with its sensual qualities, and is attached to them only through allure. In similar manner, the real object and its real qualities do not have a pre-existent bond in need of being split. Instead, they must be brought together through *fusion*, by way of some mediating term. This process, strangely akin to the allure of aesthetic experience, can be called causation. There is a precedent for this claim in the masterful treatment of efficient causation by Suárez. For him, direct causal relation between entities is impossible, and things interact only by means of their "accidents," by which he actually means their real qualities.

An even simpler way to look at the four tensions is as follows. The basis of this book are the two kinds of objects and two kinds of qualities: real and sensual in both cases. What was interesting was the realization that qualities need not marry objects of their own kind. A real object obviously needs real qualities, as Leibniz and some of the Scholastics saw. And a sensual object is always linked with shifting sensual qualities, as Husserl's phenomenology convincingly established. But there were also the two cases of exotic mixture. For real objects are associated with sensual qualities too, as seen from Heidegger's tool-analysis in which the real object hides behind its accessible surface traits. And with equal strangeness, sensual objects were also found to have real qualities, as in Husserl's insight that sensual objects have an eidos made up of genuine real qualities, as opposed to the mere shifting perceptual adumbrations whose qualities are always sensual. In this way we were shocked to discover interbreeding underway between the real and sensual realms, as if metaphysics were a Caribbean region where proper relations between objects were corrupted by rum, parrots, and volcanoes.

However, any moral outrage at this mixing of real and sensual bloodlines is beside the point, since it misses the true paradox: the vastly different ways in which real and sensual objects relate to qualities of either kind. Any sensual object is already in contact with its qualities of both kinds. The watermelon or rabid dog we experience is barely distinct either from the flickering shades by which we observe it at each moment (which we called time) or the deeper non-sensual features that the melon or dog cannot lose without ceasing to be recognized as what it is (which we called eidos). Since both of these bonds already exist, their rupture requires a fission of previously linked parts. This may sound unusual enough, but the true paradox is still to come. For let us now consider the *real* melon or dog, withdrawn from the kingdom of experience. We cannot say that these real objects have any inherent bond with their sensual qualities (the distance between them is what we called space), since these are mere appearances for someone or something else. The watermelon itself is completely indifferent to the angle or distance from which it is seen, or the precise degree of gloomy afternoon shadow in which it is shrouded. There are times when these sensual qualities are placed into orbit around the ghostly withdrawn melon (allure), but this occurs on a purely *ad hoc* basis, and the melon could hardly care less even if it were a deeply emotional creature. Thus, it is a form of fusion between previously separate poles rather than a fission of already attached poles.

But an even more paradoxical situation arises when we consider the link between the real object and its real qualities, where a more intimate bond between the two would be expected. Yet here we find that the real object has no closer link with its own real qualities than with the sensual qualities that one would never dream of ascribing to it. Once more, this is an *ad hoc* relation arising only now and then. In other words, the relation between an object and its own real qualities (we called this essence) is a relation produced by outside entities. This is not the relativist thesis according to which nothing is real, hidden, or essential but only how it appears to us. Instead, it is a bizarre alternative to relativism in which the real, hidden, and essential do very much exist, but communicate only by way of the unreal, apparent, and inessential. It would be as if mushrooms communicated with their own qualities, not directly or through rhizomal networks, but via radio waves. A real object is real and has a definite character, but its essence is first produced from the outside through causal interactions. Since this would take too long to argue in detail here, I will only observe that this strange result is required by the symmetry of our diagrams, just as certain new particles are predicted by the models of physics and confirmed only later.

FIGURE 7: Broken Links

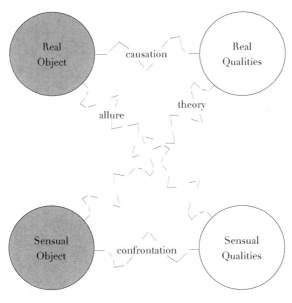

D. On Tension

Yet it is not entirely clear what a tension is, and this needs to be investigated. In the first place, it already turned out that a number of different kinds of relations are possible in the cosmos: ten of them, to be exact. But not all of these relations can really be called tensions, a term that implies simultaneous closeness and separation. For instance, multiple real or sensual qualities can exist in the same object, without this really being a tension in the sense I mean. Likewise, a perceiving agent is a real object in contact with sensual objects, and multiple sensual objects are contiguous in the experience of this agent, without any of these cases counting as tensions. What all four tensions share in common is that all involve an object-pole and a quality-pole. This section briefly considers some of the implications of this fact.

The first point, as we have already seen, is that two of the tensions can exist in something like a banal form, while the other two cannot. That is to say, a sensual object must always be accompanied by a swirling patina of sensual qualities and a not yet articulated core of real ones. Yet in both cases the tension between the object-pole and the quality-pole requires a sort of fission between the two, in which they are held side-by-side as both together and separate. It is quite different with the two tensions that involve a real object. Here, the real object is only brought together with qualities by means of fusion, so that there is actually no banal state of tension when a real rather than sensual object is involved.

The next question is why there is a "tension" in these cases rather than one of two other possible extremes. For on the one hand, two poles might be kept so entirely separate as to have no relation at all, and on the other hand they might be so fused together that a state of utterly banal attachment would be the result. We need to identify the conditions under which both extremes are able to pass into tension, whether through a fission of banality (as is the case with sensual objects) or through fusion of what was previously separate (as is the case with real ones).

8

Levels and Psyche

So far we have spoken of the world as split into two sorts of zones: the real and the sensual. This could lead to a pair of misunderstandings. The first would be to assume that the real and the sensual are two fixed sites, so that anything real would be at the bottom of the universe and anything sensual would lie at its surface. The second would be to identify the sensual with human and perhaps animal experience. In answer to the first point, there is not one special realm of real objects and another of sensual ones. Recall that the sensual is what exists only in relation to the perceiver, and that the real is whatever withdraws from that relation. But if we consider a real hammer, it is not just withdrawn from any relation that other entities might have with it. The hammer is also *composed* of relations between its component objects. And insofar as every object must have pieces (for otherwise it would be an inarticulate lump) this suggests an infinite regress of objects. And second, it is not true that the psychic pertains only to the animal. To say that not just humans but every object encounters a duel between sensual objects and their sensual qualities is not to project human psychological traits onto non-human entities. For if it turns out that every entity encounters sensual objects, such experience may bear little resemblance to the predominantly visual and intellective character of human life. While it is true that we cannot "know" what it is like to be another creature, we also cannot know the subterranean reality of a hammer, mushroom, or neutron. But this does not obstruct all knowledge about these things.

A. Levels of Objects

In the history of philosophy it is not unusual to encounter two-world theories in which everything that exists belongs to only one of the two worlds. It perhaps occurs most famously in Plato's rift between the perfect forms and the shadowy cave, and in Kant's division between the noumenal and phenomenal spheres. The split reappears in Heidegger's tool-analysis, which I have described as pivotal for object-oriented ontology. Briefly stated, there are only two places for Heidegger where entities can be found: either silently performing their labor in subterranean concealment, or sparkling before the mind in explicit presence. And while this book has tried to radicalize Heidegger's analysis through the claim that even inanimate objects reduce *each other* to presence-at-hand, it might be wondered if this is simply a more inclusive version of a two-world theory, with objects on one side and relations on the other. Yet we must oppose the theory of two worlds: not in order to flatten everything onto a single plane of immanence, but because object and relations are not two fixed points on a map. Instead, every entity has two sides. Rather than a two-world theory we should speak instead of a two-*face* theory, a philosophy born under the proverbial sign of Janus.

Consider the case of Leibniz, who draws an unfortunate distinction between substance and aggregate. Individual entities such as diamonds, people, horses, and trees might be said to have monads. The same is not true for Leibniz's "aggregates" or "things of reason," which lack the supposed real unity of natural things. Examples of such aggregates would include two diamonds glued together, a circle of men holding hands, a cavalry regiment, and the Black Forest as a whole. In short, Leibniz's own version of the two-world theory functions as a taxonomy applied to *specific* entities, assigning them to one neighborhood of the cosmos or the other. Now it might seem that Heidegger's theory avoids this, since the same hammer can be considered as belonging to both worlds, *Zuhandenheit* and *Vorhandenheit*. But the problem remains that Heidegger allows for nothing deeper than the being of a thing. If we consider the hammer in its sequestered tool-being, we find it already at the bottom of the universe. We are thus left with nothing but a permanent play of light and shadow across a *single* gap between genuine being and derivative presence, and with human experience as the sole site of presence. But this theory is false. I have gladly followed Heidegger in distinguishing between the hammer in its presence-at-hand and its withdrawal into shadow. Nevertheless, the subterranean hammer is no ultimate basement of the cosmos. Although the hammer is certainly deeper than any relations that other objects might have with it, it is also formed of relations in its own right.

In other words, it is not enough to think of an object as existing in two forms: first in itself, and second as it appears in any relation. Instead, the object is a walled island that differs from relations in both directions. For just as the hammer withdraws from any specific contact that humans or other entities might have with it, so too the hammer emerges from the components of which it is built. To reduce the hammer to its outward relations would overmine it, reducing it to a Husserlian phenomenon or Latourian actor that exists only in relation with other things. Conversely, to call the hammer nothing but a nickname for its sum total of pieces would *undermine* it, reducing it to nothing more than an epiphenomenon of its material ancestry. Hence it should now be clear that the hammer as a real tool-being is not located in the basement of the universe at all, since a layer of constituent pieces swarms beneath it, another layer beneath that one, and so forth. Instead of saying that this regress into constituent objects is indefinite, I would go so far as to call it infinite, in spite of the ban found in Kant's Antinomies on ruling either for or against an infinite regress of pieces. After all, to be real means to have a multitude of qualities, both real and perceived. And given that an object must inherently be a unity, its multitude of qualities can only arise from the plurality of its pieces. Thus there is no object without pieces, and an infinite regress occurs. Despite the easy and widespread mockery of the infinite regress, there are only two alternatives, and both are even worse. Instead of the infinite regress we can have *a finite regress*, in which one ultimate element is the material of everything larger. Or we can have *no regress at all*, in which there is no depth behind what appears to the human mind. Both options have already been critiqued as undermining and overmining, respectively. And if the infinite regress is often mocked as a theory of "turtles all the way down," the finite regress merely worships a final Almighty Turtle, while the theory of no regress champions a world resting on a turtle shell without a turtle.

Just as the hammer is not the basement of the universe, human perception of that hammer need not be the roof. It is often assumed that the human relation to reality is one of transcendence. Whereas inanimate entities seem trapped in the turmoil of the world, humans are believed to rise above that world into a windy, starry space of freedom where they lucidly observe things "as" what they are. But this is not the case. For notice that our relation with an entity can itself become a unified object that withdraws from the scrutiny of all other entities, including we ourselves: as when we form marriages and business partnerships, or join the Foreign Legion. The implications of these links are by no means fully accessible to their participants. Human consciousness does not transcend the cosmos and observe it from a neutral scientific void, but forever burrows through an intermediate layer of reality, no more aware of the larger objects to which it belongs than of the tool-beings that withdraw from it. Nonetheless, despite the infinite regress downward, it will be shown later that there is no infinite progress upward. If we imagine the universe as an ocean, it would be an ocean without a floor, but with a turbulent surface of objects and nothing but empty sky above.

FIGURE 8: The Four Tensions

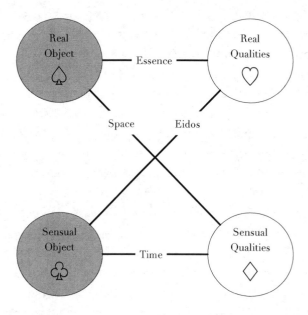

FIGURE 9: The Three Radiations

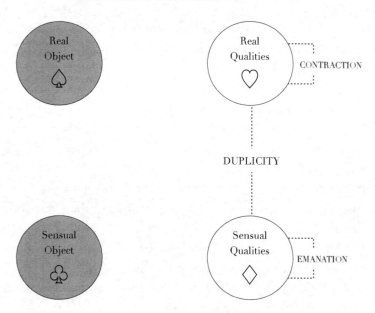

FIGURE 10: The Three Junctions

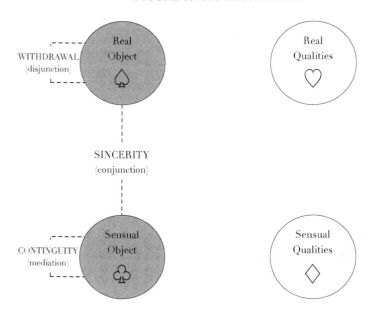

B. The Interiors of Objects

When Brentano reintroduced the medieval term "intention-ality," he also made use of its longer form: "intentional inexis-tence." In this context inexistence does not mean "nonexis-tence," but the existence of something on the interior of something else. Namely, every mental act contains an object as that toward which it is directed. For Brentano only mental reality contains an object, and this distinguishes it from the physical. The same holds for Brentano's student Husserl, who leaves even less room for physical reality than his teacher. Now, I certainly endorse the notion of immanent objectivity: one of the pillars of this book is the sensual object, which exists only insofar as it is intended. And yet it is necessary to modify the views of Brentano and Husserl on this point. There are two reasons for this. First, the location of sensual objects cannot be inside the mind, since both the mind *and* its sensual objects are located on the interior of a more encompassing object. If I perceive a tree, this sensual object and I do not meet up inside my mind, and for a simple reason: my mind and its object are two equal partners in the intention, and the unifying term must contain both. The mind cannot serve as both part and whole simultaneously. Instead, both the mind and its object are encompassed by something larger: namely, both exist inside the object formed through the relation between me and the *real* tree, which may be rather different from the trees found in everyday life. Second, Brentano's view that physical entities have no immanent objects while mental entities do is just a case of wrongly ascribing two different ontological structures to two separate *kinds* of beings. We can call this the Taxonomic Fallacy. For it would be more accurate to say that physical things and minds are both objects. And qua objects, both withdraw from any relations and simply perform the labor of being what they are. Insofar as they do relate to other things, they confront objects that are not immanent in themselves as privileged mental agents, but immanent in the larger objects into which they have entered. We can take these points one at a time.

First, we need to abandon several prejudices concerning objects. There is a strong tendency to think of them primarily as bulky physical solids. And since these sorts of things normally have a certain durability, we tend to think of objects as needing tenacity over time. Again following the model of physical things, we generally like objects to have a certain homogeneity. That is to say, we are rarely bothered if a rock is called an object despite containing billions of different atoms, but more bothered if someone speaks of the European Union as an object despite the great variation of its components. But there are no grounds for this bias. For the purposes of this book, an object is anything that has a unified reality that is autonomous from its wider context and also from its own pieces. If a hammer were nothing more than the various uses to which it were put, then it would merely be a hammer-image rather than a hammer. By the same token, if a hammer were nothing more than its pieces, it would merely be a pile of molecules rather than a hammer. But while it cannot exist without these molecules, it can also withstand certain changes in their arrangement without ceasing to be the same hammer — a principle sometimes known as redundant causation.[56]

These points are meant to fend off any incredulity toward what I am about to say: namely, *any relation immediately generates a new object.* If certain components are arranged in such a manner as to give rise to a thing that exceeds them, in such a way that it can withstand certain changes in these components, then they have entered a genuine relation with each other as real objects rather than merely stroking one another's sensual facades. It should now be clear that insofar as we somehow connect with a real object outside us, giving rise to perceptions of sensual trees, mailboxes, or blackbirds, we have somehow linked with that object to form a new real object. While it is true that perceptions are transient, not purely physical, and also made up of rather heterogeneous pieces, these points disqualify them as objects only for those who accept needless traditional views of what an object is. For in fact, my perception of a tree does meet the criteria for an object. It is definitely unified, for it is one perception. It is also something new, irreducible to its pieces in isolation, since neither I nor the tree in a vacuum give rise to anything like a tree-perception. And furthermore, this perception of a tree has a reality deeper than any attempt to describe it, which is precisely why phenomenological practice is so tricky. But if my relation with a tree forms a new object, then I as a real piece of that object find myself on its interior, confronting the mere image of the other piece.

Thus we find an asymmetry on the interior of the object, between the real me and the sensual tree. The duality is inescapable: there is always a non-transitive contact in which a real object caresses merely sensual ones. If the tree relates to me as well, this must happen on the interior of a separate but related object. The usual mistake lies in obeying the Taxonomic Fallacy — the assumption that this asymmetry results from the inter-section between two different *kinds* of entities. Under this assumption, "mind" will always be the real object while "body" is doomed to appear as a phantom before the mind, never able to perceive in its own right. But in fact, physical bodies do encounter other entities, and they cannot drain those entities to the dregs any more than a human mind can. Hence, the true duality is not between minds and bodies, but between real and sensual objects. Real stones and trees must encounter sensual incarnations of other entities in some primitive fashion. But this inevitably leads to worries over the dangers of panpsychism.

C. On Panpsychism

Normally there seems to be an unbridgeable gulf between human beings and inanimate objects such as rocks or flames. Humans are not just physically located in the world, and do not just inflict and receive blows. Instead, we also have some explicit awareness of our predicament in the world. This seems to give humans a special ontological status as a tear in the fabric of the world, a flaw in the cosmic jewel. Somehow, through some sort of tragedy or magic spell, human thought rises above the mere exchange of physical blows in such a way that other entities become present to it. This is perhaps the key point of consensus in philosophy since Kant. In the wake of his so-called Copernican Revolution, philosophers may disagree about whether there is a reality lying beyond us, but most are agreed that the human-world relation is the basis for all others, or at least for knowing about the others. The collision of hailstones and ocean, assuming that no humans are there to observe it, is not granted the same ontological status as that between humans and ocean. This standpoint generally dodges the question of animals, whose mental life is left stranded somewhere between blind mechanism and full human transcendence. There have been various attempts to explain the nature of animal mentality as a privation of human cognition, such as claiming that "language" or the "as-structure" is what makes us different. But it is safe to say that these attempts shed little light on the problem: Heidegger's famous 1929/30 lectures,[57] for instance, say nothing useful about the "world-poverty" of the animal that they proudly proclaim.

By contrast, object-oriented ontology holds that the human-world relation has no privilege at all. Thanks to Whitehead, who posited the single category of "prehension" as a primitive form of relation from which all others are built, Kant's human-world duopoly is faced with a serious rival. The usual rejoinders to this emerging rival teach us little. They generally amount to sarcastic remarks such as: "I happen to think that human perception of this table is different from what happens to a rock when lying on top of it," or: "Let me know when you teach a parrot to ask why there is something rather than nothing." Snide objections of this sort miss the point for a simple reason: no one is claiming that inanimate entities possess the full human toolbox of mental abilities, including such talents as language, emotion, cognition, foresight, or dreams. There is no evidence that trees and houses write poetry, suffer nervous breakdowns, or learn from their mistakes. The question is whether this obvious difference between humans and non-humans deserves to be made into a *basic ontological rift*. For we are merely biased if we assume that humans are a decisive rupture in the world. The difference between people and minerals is vast indeed, but so is that between stars and black holes, or hunter-gatherers and string theorists. The point is to avoid the Taxonomic Fallacy of assuming that basic ontological divides can be identified with specific *kinds* of entities.

Instead, the basic rift in the cosmos lies between objects and relations in general: between their autonomous reality outside all relation, and their caricatured form in the sensual life of other objects. Whatever the special features of plants, fungi, animals, and humans may be, they are simply complex forms of the gap between objects and relations, just as heavier chemical elements arise from hydrogen and helium. By no means does this imply that mentality is reducible to neuroscience or string physics. For our principles forbid that any specific kind of entity could be the building block for everything else in the cosmos. Instead, everything plays out in the strife between concealed objects and the twisted or translated forms in which they appear to other objects. This does sound like panpsychism, a doctrine widely viewed as absurd in our post-Kantian atmosphere of human privilege. But panpsychism is currently in the midst of a rehabilitation. This can be seen with especial clarity in David Skrbina's masterful survey *Panpsychism in the West*,[58] a book that does at least two important things. First, Skrbina shows that panpyschism has never been just the deviant fantasy of laughable crackpots, but can be found almost everywhere in the philosophy of the West (to say nothing of Asia). Second, Skrbina observes that panpsychism has no need to project special human traits onto rocks and atoms. In fact, philosophy needs a more dedicated speculation on the different levels of psyche at different levels of objects: a still nonexistent field that I like to call "speculative psychology."

The basis for panpsychism has nothing to do with a romantic conception of sensitive plants or weeping minerals. Instead, it emerges directly from rejection of the Kantian Revolution. If all relations are on the same footing, and all relations are equally inept at exhausting the depths of their terms, then an intermediate form of contact between things must be possible. This contact can only take a *sensual* form, since it can only encounter translated or distorted versions of other objects. Complaining that objects do not encounter others "as" objects solves nothing as long as no clarification is given of what the "as" means.

Perhaps fire does not think about the cotton that it burns, and perhaps it feels no guilt or pity over its violent actions. But the fire still makes indirect contact with the cotton, since direct contact is impossible (as the Ash'arite occasionalists first saw). This leaves the sensual realm as the only possible field of contact, difficult though it may be to imagine the secret inner life of fire. More controversially, I also hold that the sensual world of inanimate objects does not encounter mere bundles of qualities, but also faces the Husserlian rift between sensual objects and adumbrations no less than humans do.

D. On Polypsychism

The rift between sensual objects and their qualities is not a special feature of human intellect or animal sentience, but a basic feature of relationality in general. For once we see that all objects encounter a sensual realm of caricatures, there are only two alternatives to such a rift. We could say that they encounter either a colorful swarm of disjoined qualities, or unitary lumps of inarticulate pulp. The first alternative fails since qualities cannot be encountered in a vacuum, but are always emanated or emitted from some sensual object: the green of a bush, the black of a hangman's hood. Even inanimate objects do not react to all the data available to them; minute fluctuations in the surface of a table may affect a paperweight in some way without the paperweight ceasing to encounter it as a table. The second alternative fails for an even simpler reason: namely, sensual objects without specific qualitative character would be nonsensical. The paperweight is supported by a table, not by a "sensual object in general," since otherwise there would be no reason for it to sit on the table rather than being melted or flying off into space. The remaining option is the true one: the rift between sensual objects and their qualities is not a special poignant feature of animal or human mentality, but belongs to the very structure of relation. By considering the possible variations in this rift, a speculative psychology might one day emerge, leading philosophy to the tectonic plates that separate atoms from gold, moss, mosquitoes, Neanderthals, and bears.

Yet despite my insistence that panpsychism should not be mocked, I cannot defend its use of the prefix pan-, or "all." Hence I will speak of *polypsychism*, in order to stress that the roster of experiencing entities must indeed balloon beyond all previous limits, but without quite extending to *all* entities. This is not because of some wish to exclude a handful of despicable objects from the democratic expansion of souls: as if dust, cockroaches, and empty plastic bottles were to be exiled to a philosophical slum while flowers and electrons are granted the honors of psyche. For we must always avoid the Taxonomic Fallacy by not distributing the terms "perceiving" and "non-perceiving" among specific *kinds* of entities. Instead, perceiving and non-perceiving must be found in the same entity at different times; they are modes of being rather than types of object. The important point is that objects do not perceive insofar as they *exist*, as panpsychism proclaims. Instead, they perceive insofar as they *relate*. Recall that to perceive means to encounter sensual objects on the interior of a larger object, and that a real entity is located on such an interior thanks to a relation that makes it a *component* of that more encompassing object. But there is no reason to think that all objects find themselves in such relations at any given moment. While it is true that a real object arises from a descending chain of countless smaller components, it does not follow that it must also enter further relations as a component of larger objects: just as an animal's long unbroken list of ancestors does not mean that it will reproduce successfully in its own right. The cosmos has no bottom, but does have a surface. There may be an infinite regress, but no infinite progress: no final, encompassing object that could be called a universe.

In short, not all objects perceive at all times; some objects are sleeping, or *dormant*. The metaphor is suggestive even if human sleep is never a perfect cessation of awareness or relation. Dreams enter the mind of a sleeper, as do the vague impressions of distant bells or servants entering the room. But the sleep of a dormant object would instead be a state of perfect sleep, in which an entity would be real without entering into further relations at all. Note that this would be nothing like death: the dead object is no longer real, while the dormant object is real but simply without relation. An object is real when it forms an autonomous unit able to withstand certain changes in its pieces. This does not require additional relations with other entities, since we have seen that the real object lies *deeper* than such relations, and often enters them with no lasting effect to itself. In this respect, dormant objects are the purest kind of object we can study. They are not altogether lonely, since they do have pieces; they are simply not pieces of anything else, and therefore they do not perceive. In principle some objects might remain dormant forever. They might be perfectly real without ever being discovered, caressed, or capitalized upon in such a way as to enter into a higher object, like drops of water forever at the surface of the ocean. But it remains to be seen how a dormant object could suddenly awaken and enter into relations if no relations were present before.

The basic model of object-oriented philosophy is now before the reader. There are two kinds of objects (real and sensual) and two kinds of qualities (also real and sensual). These four poles of reality are not isolated, but always locked in a duel with one another according to various permutations. Among them are four that involve a special tension between one object-pole and one quality-pole, and these have been named time, space, essence, and eidos. Although numerous riddles and paradoxes arise from this model, paradox is the most convincing evidence of its value.

9

Ontography

We have outlined a model that contains four poles: two kinds of object, and two kinds of quality. Our task is now as follows. We must consider the various possible combinations of these poles to see how they interact, and must also show that the model is both compelling and fruitful. If not compelling, then it will resemble just another amateur or crackpot system of the world. If not fruitful, then it will be nothing but a sterile exercise in structural abstraction. Kant did not merely carve the world into categories, but tried to show how they could be applied to topics of persistent interest to human beings. Freud did not merely determine that dreams are wish fulfillments and then say nothing more, but developed this insight into a complete theory of mental illness and ultimately of human culture in general. Any philosophy worthy of the name should be in quest of a similar degree of fertility.

For any group that contains four elements, ten permutations should be possible in principle. Consider the case of playing cards, which obviously come in four suits. A diamond card might be paired with another diamond, or with a heart, club, or spade. But these are merely the formal possibilities; there may be further restrictions in the real world that make certain combinations impossible. A name is needed for the exercise of describing and classifying such pairings, and to this end I select a word that was invented in a spirit of mockery rather than admiration. In a classic ghost story, the English writer M.R. James describes a particular university pedant as a "Professor of Ontography."[59] A quick Google search indicates that the word "ontography" has occasionally been proposed in recent decades for serious endeavors. But in none of these cases does the word seem to have caught on; hence it is still up for grabs, and we can borrow James's term for the topic to be described in the present section. Rather than a geography dealing with stock natural characters such as forests and lakes, ontography maps the basic landmarks and fault lines in the universe of objects.

A. Sorting the Families

As an additional tool we can add some abbreviations to the mix. Although too much shorthand in philosophy can give the distracting impression of a sterile technical exercise, a small amount of abbreviation can spare us the burden of always referring to the four poles of the world by their lengthier names. In this spirit, we have already used "RO" to stand for real object, "RQ" for real quality, "SO" for sensual object, and "SQ" for sensual quality. For the sake of vividness, we will also remain with the metaphor of playing cards. Just as there are two red and two black suits in a standard deck of cards, ontography recognizes two "suits" of objects and two of qualities. This image will make it easier to imagine how different sorts of pairings break down into families. First, we note that there are four different ways of pairing red suits with black, and hence four ways of pairing object with quality: namely RO-RQ, RO-SQ, SO-SQ, and SO-RQ. Since all of these pairings match object with quality, they can be called heterogeneous pairs, with four distinct possible weddings of red and black. Likewise, there are three possible pairings of each color with itself. For instance, in the case of red we can have hearts with hearts, diamonds with diamonds, or hearts with diamonds. In terms of ontography this would be manifest as RQ-RQ, SQ-SQ, and RQ-SQ. Similarly, the black suits can be combined as spade-spade, club-club, or spade-club, which ontography describes as RO-RO, SO-SO, and RO-SO. In this way, we can adopt the initial hypothesis that these are the three basic families of polarization in the world.

We can see what results from this supposition, and make modifications later if necessary.

So far most of our attention has been drawn by the heterogeneous pairs, which were introduced with the suggestive names of *time, space, essence, and eidos*. They mark four great tensions in the world, and their names suggest a certain link with the basic features of the physical and metaphysical realms. We also saw that for each tension there is a special way to place object and quality in explicit counterpoint. "Confrontation" turns the unspoken duel of sensual object and quality found in time into an open dispute between its two constituents. "Allure" plays an analogous role for space, "causation" for essence, and "theory" for eidos. It was also noted that these four tensions break down into two sub-families, since two of them involve an always available sensual object, while the other two are concerned with the real object that withdraws into inscrutable depths. The sensual object cannot possibly exist except in tension with its sensual qualities (time) and its real qualities (eidos), insofar as the sensual object is never something truly autonomous. Normally it exists in easy union with its qualities, since regular perception makes no explicit distinction between the tree and its shimmering surface features or real subterranean notes. What is required in these cases, if anything new is ever to happen, is *fission* between the two poles. The opposite holds for the real object, which is not initially in any sort of tension with the surface qualities that announce it (space) or the multitude of features belonging to it (essence). In these two cases, *fusion* is required between the real object and its real or sensual qualities; in its own right, it has no dealings with these parasitical clouds of features. All four of these processes need more detailed description. And furthermore, we also need to know what causes such fission or fusion to occur.

The nature of the red pairs is not nearly so complicated as when red and black are mixed. For it is obvious that all of them involve qualities: RQ-RQ, SQ-SQ, and RQ-SQ. Now, there is only one pole of the world that could possibly serve as the bond between such qualities: the object to which they belong. Two real or two sensual qualities are linked only insofar as they both belong to the same object. And while it might seem logical that real qualities are linked through real objects and sensual qualities through sensual ones, the rule turns out not to be so strict. Initially, both kinds of qualities are linked only through *sensual* objects. Recall Husserl's discovery that an intentional object is a unit not only by comparison with its accidental surface features, but is also unified over against its real eidetic qualities, which can never be grasped through sensuous intuition. For instance, as I observe a tree it is merely a sensual object. Yet this object has both shifting accidental features that can be extensively shuffled without annihilating the sensual tree, and durable real qualities that the sensual tree needs in order to be what it is. Any sensual object exists only in constant strife with both kinds of features, which belong to it and yet do not belong. Only in special cases of fusion can either sort of quality seem to become attached to a real object. In the banal state of things, the RQ-RQ and SQ-SQ pairs are both mediated by a sensual object.

In the latter case, SQ-SQ, it might initially seem to be the observer who binds them, since we have seen that a sensual apple or dog exists only for one who encounters it. But recall that the observer has no direct contact with sensual qualities at all. This is merely the empiricist dogma rejected by Husserl, who shows that we are always in contact with sensual objects, and that qualities are merely derivative of these objects. In the case of sensual qualities, they are indirectly linked insofar as they *emanate* together from the same sensual object, to use a famous neo-Platonic term. We have seen that for the most part, real qualities exist only in a link with a sensual object. But this cannot be described as emanation, since these qualities are in no way emitted into view. Thus, a more appropriate term for real qualities in their link with sensual objects would be Nicholas of Cusa's famous *contraction*. The remaining pair, RQ-SQ, has already been described in passing when discussing sensual objects such as the tree. Namely, the tree has both real and sensual qualities at any given moment, perhaps quite different from each other. For this reason the RQ-SQ pair can be known by the name of *duplicity*.

We now turn to the black pairs: RO-RO, SO-SO, and RO-SO. They are a motlier family than the reds, since each has very different aspects. Let's begin with the pairing of sensual objects. We already know that sensual objects are linked only through their *contiguity* in the same field of experience for a single observer: I encounter not just one sensual object at a time, but many. As for the bond between two real objects, the founding principle of object-oriented philosophy is the insight that such objects make no direct link whatsoever. In this way Heidegger's notion of veiled tool-beings combines with Whitehead's cosmological vision of all interactions being on the same level, so that inanimate entities are concealed from each other no less than from us. If two sensual objects can never be anything better than contiguous, two real objects co-exist in the manner of *withdrawal*, having no interrelation at all. The entire metaphysics of vicarious causation is designed to shed light on this issue. That leaves only the RO-SO pair, which we have called the *sincerity* of immediate contact. Here, the experiencer as a real object is in direct contact with a sensual object.

In this way we have mapped the ten possible forms of tension within the world. The mixed-color tensions are the ones we called time, space, essence, and eidos. The red pairs, or radiations, are called emanation, contraction, and duplicity. And the black pairs, or junctions, shall be known as withdrawal, contiguity, and sincerity. But this schema of ten categories is unfamiliar enough that it obviously stands in need of further clarification.

B. The Red and the Black: Tensions

The metaphors drawn from card games may prove useful for making our model more vivid. Consider the case of recent physics and QCD, or "Quantum Chromodynamics," a theory of how the strong nuclear force arises from the interaction between quarks. While there is nothing truly colorful at such a tiny level of the cosmos, the employment of the primary colors red, blue, and green provides a strong intuitive basis for an otherwise rather technical model of the strong nuclear force. By analogy, instead of our always speaking of "real objects" or "sensual qualities," it will be helpful to have a set of intuitive synonyms for these terms and their interplay. In our case just one pair of colors (red and black) is needed to account for the various poles, though just as with cards we have two suits of each color. While the decision of which color to use for which is somewhat arbitrary, in past writings I have referred to qualities as "black noise" emanating from objects — which can also be considered as "black boxes" of a sort. For this reason I prefer to use the black suits to refer to the object-poles and the red ones to the quality-poles. And though it might sound flippant at first, it can be refreshing to speak of the object as exemplifying four different modes, just as we speak of four different suits for each number of card, whether it be a Jack or any other. In the case of a dog, for instance, we could speak charmingly of the Dog of Clubs (the sensual object), Dog of Diamonds (its sensual qualities), Dog of Spades (the real object), and Dog of Hearts (its real qualities). But this is meant only as a whimsical image that adds useful synonyms to our arsenal, and is by no means proposed as grave technical terminology.

The first task with these heterogeneous pairs is to describe their everyday state of banality, as opposed to those special events in which object and quality exist side by side. What we find is that two of our pairs (SO-SQ, SO-RQ, yielding time and eidos) are already attached in normal experience, while the others (RO-RQ, RO-SQ, yielding essence and space) are not united unless their connection is *produced*. The banal state of time and eidos is this: object and qualities seem compressed into a unit, and only in special cases do they appear in explicit strife: fission, as we have called it. The opposite holds for essence and space, where the real object is never counterposed with its sensual and real qualities except in the case of their fusion. For it is not at all the case that space is constantly with us in experience: rather, experience is a kind of hologram in which all near and distant objects touch us directly and spatial distance is merely inferred. And though it may sound surprising at first, it is also not the case that a real object has an articulated essence, because its essence is produced only once in awhile. So much for the banal state of things.

Yet the next question is why such banal circumstances are ever ruptured at all. Alain Badiou holds that rare truth-events are needed to rupture the mediocre "state of the situation." We join him entirely in adopting this principle, and also in making such events four in number.[60] Of course, the nature of the splits is completely different in his case and ours, and neither does Badiou allow for inanimate objects as well as humans to be the subjects of such events. If there are times when a real or sensual object separates from its qualities and unites with new ones, we need to know when and why this happens. This is no artificial question, but touches on the key philosophical problem of why anything happens at all: why not sheer stasis instead? What is inadequate about the current configuration of things that makes it undergo turbulent change, and only sometimes rather than always? Even if the bond between an object and its qualities is clearly somewhat loose, we still must wonder why the object might suddenly eject or absorb them. In several respects the model of ontography has begun to resemble that of particle physics.

The third question that must be posed about time, space, essence, and eidos is whether these four pairs of objects and qualities touch one another directly, or whether some mediator is needed. In two of the cases (space and essence) the answer is simple: mediation is required by some other term. After all, in these cases the objects and qualities are separate by definition: fusion between these poles is required, and some middle term must do the fusing. The situation is less certain in the case of time and eidos, since here the sensual object is always already in contact with both its sensual and real qualities. Yet given that sensual objects exist in the first place only for some experiencing entity, there is good reason to say that this experiencing entity is the third term able to bridge the gap between two separate poles.

And this brings us to the final question, not raised until now: what exactly is a quality? Given Husserl's claim that qualities must emanate from an underlying sensual object, it seems impossible that they should be universals: for if blue is always a different color in the case of equal-hued ocean, sky, shirt, eyes, and paint, then universals are always a second-order abstraction, not the very stuff of the senses. For related reasons it remains unclear how sensual qualities differ from sensual objects, given that there no longer seems to be any purely given sense data in experience, since qualities are always siphoned from objects. If I turn my attention to the supposed qualities of an object, what I find are further objects, not raw qualia. Then qualities are not a chaotic white noise, but a "black noise" drawn from the objects that make up the pieces of any given sensual object. And finally, if it is true that all experienced qualities are laden with theories about the objects around which they orbit, we need to know if there is really any difference between sensual qualities and real ones.

C. The Red and the Red: Radiations

We now come to the quality-quality pairs called "red," as when diamonds consort with diamonds, real qualities with sensual ones, or any other such combination. Here again, we first need to know about the state of banality of these pairings: what is the *normal* interaction between each of these things when paired with a pole or suit of its own kind? In the case of any pairing of qualities, it is obvious that their normal state of existence is to be bound together in the same object: the multiple accidents of a sensual tree belong together only through the mediation of the tree, and the same holds for its numerous real qualities. However, there is an important difference in the two kinds of qualities. We have seen that sensual objects always exist in conjunction with such qualities, and are split from them only in the relatively rare case of fission. By contrast, real objects take on a plurality of essential features only in cases of fusion, and in this sense their state of banality means not being connected at all. An analogous feature occurs in the case of the two kinds of objects. Multiple sensual objects coexist in advance for the same experiencing agent, and thereby their banal state is to be contiguous or linked for the agent who experiences them. But this does not hold for real objects, whose mode of being is to be disconnected from each other in advance. In short, we find that banal connection between one pole and another is found only in experience, not in withdrawn genuine reality.

The next question will be when and why these pairs unite and divide. In the case of real or sensual qualities, this turns out to be nothing but a byproduct of one of the heterogeneous pairings. Consider the case of two real qualities linked in a single real object. We have seen that this requires a kind of fusion that we have called essence, and linked with the phenomenon of causation. Something rather different happens in the case of two sensual qualities, which are always already linked with a sensual object, and hence do not need to contract into the object, since they *emanate* from it at the outset. The only way for these qualities to lose their link through the sensual object is for a split to occur between the sensual object and its qualities, which we called *confrontation*.

The third question is what, if anything, mediates these red pairs? But here the answers are fairly obvious, since we have already covered them briefly. We know that both real and sensual qualities are always bound together only by the same sensual object. We also know that the same holds true for any mixed combination of real and sensual qualities, which are bound together in the same sensual object: the real traits of a sunflower paired with its shimmering accidents in one and the same sensual flower.

But the final question here is somewhat different from that in the previous section. Namely, why are we dealing with multiplicities here at all? Why is it that a sensual tree has numerous *different* sensual qualities, and a real dog has numerous *different* real qualities? The answer, I propose, comes from the fact that any real or sensual object is made up of multiple pieces. When these pieces join together to form the object in question, the excessive properties of the parts that are not needed by the interaction are left over, as a sort of gas or aroma of qualities surrounding the object — an industrial byproduct of the process through which it was fabricated. The same holds in a different way for the relation between real objects and real qualities as well: for even if a real object is not attached to its multiple qualities in the same way as a sensual one is, those qualities need to be filtered through some real object to be available for possible use later on.

D. The Black and the Black: Junctions

We now move to the final triad of pairs: RO-RO, SO-SO, and RO-SO, in which different kinds of objects somehow combine. Our first question again concerns the state of everyday banality of these pairs. As concerns the link between a real object and a sensual one, the normal state is obviously one of immediate contact; we have seen that experience is nothing other than this confrontation of an experiencing real object with a sensual one.

At the same time, the RO-RO pairing of real objects (given their difficulty of making contact) is another anomaly that perhaps belongs with RO-SO in a final category of oddities. Meanwhile, we know that the SO-SO pair exists only in a state of contiguity for the same real object who experiences these sensual objects at once.

But staying with the current morphologically assigned pairs for the moment, we again need to ask when and why they unite and divide. And here we encounter another anomaly in the case of the pairing of real and sensual objects. Though the real object is in contact with a sensual one, no fission is possible here, precisely because there is no mediator between the two poles for whom fission could possibly occur. A sincerity cannot be subjected to fission. The only thing that can be done to sincerity is simply to end it: replacing it with a new sincerity or even with nothing, as in the cases of sleep or outright death. When sincerity ceases, no mediator is present to experience this event, and hence it merely vanishes from the cosmos. There is no second witness to sincerity.

The third question, here as always, is what mediates the poles in this category. When real objects face sensual ones in sincerity, RO-SO, the answer is obviously "nothing." Their contact is direct: the only case of direct contact we know. And if RO-SO is a direct contact, the RO-RO kind is neither direct nor mediated, but simply does not occur, which is why vicarious causation is required in the first place. That leaves us with the easiest case of the three: SO-SO contact, which we have already seen is mediated by the real experiencing object that simultaneously encounters both sensual ones.

The fourth and final question is different here, just as it was different in the previous two sections. We now have a pairing of sensual objects with real ones where contact is immediate or direct. And alongside this we have the pairing of real objects with real ones, which obviously must occur given the emergence of compound objects, but occurs neither directly nor through any short-distance mediation. It must occur in some much more mediated or complicated manner. The question is why one of these pairs makes mutual contact when the other cannot: a strange complementary relation, even if a structurally pleasing one. We have already said why two real objects cannot touch directly: because they cannot encounter each other in anything but proxy form. But there remains the question of why a real object touches a sensual one at all: what does this teach us about the structure of the cosmos and of objects? Having done much preliminary work to develop ontography into a reasonably plausible discipline, we must now try to reap the rewards. We need a more detailed atlas of all possible interactions between the poles of the world, and it must be one that yields fruit.

10

Speculative Realism

Most recent philosophy in the continental tradition can safely be described as a Philosophy of Access to the world. Concurring with the spirit of Žižek's principle that "Kant was the first philosopher," it assumes that the human-world gap is the privileged site of all rigorous philosophy. This remains true even when (or *especially* when) it denies any unbridgeable gap between these two poles, making them mutually co-determining. We have seen that in 2006, Meillassoux gave this position the memorable name of "correlationism." However this term was received in France, in the Anglophone world it served as the catalyst for a new philosophical movement known as Speculative Realism. The public debut of this movement occurred in London in April 2007,[61] and it has proven wildly popular among the younger generation of continental philosophers in the United Kingdom and North America. Still, the Speculative Realist group was characterized mostly by a shared enemy: mainstream correlationist philosophy. In other respects, intellectual fault lines were present in the group from the start, and none of the original members aside from me can be called an "object-oriented philosopher"[62] in any sense of the term.

Of the original Speculative Realists, only Meillassoux avoids outright hostility to correlationism. Despite his critique of this position, his aim is not to abolish it, but to radicalize it from within, thereby pursuing a form of absolute knowledge. This can be seen most clearly in his defense of Fichte at the inaugural Speculative Realism conference.[63] As Meillassoux put it then:

By the term "correlation," I also wanted to exhibit the essential argument of these "philosophies of access," as Harman calls them; and — I insist on this point — the exceptional strength of this argumentation, apparently and desperately implacable. Correlationism rests on an argument as simple as it is powerful, and which can be formulated in the following way: No X without givenness of X, and no theory about X without a positing of X. If you speak about something, you speak about something that is given to you, and posited by you.[64]

In Section 4D of the present book, I gave reasons for why I cannot follow this line of argument; our differences should now be clear enough. Whereas I greatly lament that Kant's things-in-themselves were abandoned by German Idealism, Meillassoux actually celebrates the amputation of the unknowable in-itself as the genuine road to a rationalist philosophy. In this respect he shares much in common with Badiou and Žižek, his fellow champions of a "post-finitude" model of knowledge. By contrast, my own complaint about Kant is not that he preserved the things-in-themselves, but rather that he saw them as haunting human knowledge alone rather than relationality more generally. Like Whitehead I hold that the in-itself is real. Yet I also hold that this reality remains unattained by inanimate causal relations no less than by human subjects. For there is, in fact, a cotton-in-itself that withdraws from fire no less than from human awareness.

Unlike Meillassoux, Ray Brassier (Beirut) and Iain Hamilton Grant (Bristol) share my distaste for placing the human-world correlate at the basis of philosophy, even if in radicalized form. These two oppose my position for a different reason: while endorsing realism, they reject my "object-oriented" version of it. In Grant's case this is because of his undermining attitude toward objects, influenced by the works of Schelling and

Deleuze.[65] For Grant, individual entities arise only when deeper productive forces are obstructed or retarded by barriers of some sort. The dynamism in the world comes from a formless "productivity" rather than from individual objects. In the case of Brassier, who is deeply devoted to scientific naturalism, objects are not genuine personae in the world, but merely remnants of an archaic "folk ontology" that views the world in commonsensical terms as made up of solid mid-sized objects.[66] Although Brassier follows cognitive science in rejecting consciousness as an autonomous sphere lying outside the material world, he is also not a "realist" in my sense of the term, given that he accepts no fundamental rift between reality and the conditions under which it is known by science. For Brassier as for Meillassoux (though for different reasons) the world can ultimately be mathematized, and hence truth does not require the oblique approach on which I insist, since for them reality is in principle commensurate with knowledge.

This summary means to suggest that rather than a philosophical movement in the strict sense, Speculative Realism was the cradle for four very different philosophical trends. As a representative of the object-oriented splinter group, I would like to close these pages with a reprisal of why I defend objects as the root of all philosophy. This position is drawn from my reading of phenomenology, a historical current less admired by my three comrades. First, I think that objects cannot be reduced to anything else, and must be addressed by philosophy on their own terms. Second, the tensions between objects and their qualities and other objects can be used to account for anything else that exists; it is truly a global subject matter. Third, I hold that the object-oriented model holds great promise for many domains of knowledge, but especially for the various disciplines in the humanities.

A. Objects and Realism

We have seen that one of the worst effects of phenomenology (a movement I have always cherished) was to cement the notion that the dispute between realism and anti-realism is a "pseudo-problem." Since intentionality is always directed toward something outside itself, perceiving or hating some object, phenomenology supposedly gives us all the realism we will ever need, and without falling into the "naive" realism that posits entities beyond all possible perception. The problem is that the objects of intentionality are by no means real, as proven by the fact that we hate, love, or fear many things that turn out not to exist in the least. By confining itself to sensual objects and leaving no room for real ones, phenomenology is idealist to the core, and cannot get away with dismissing as a "pseudo-problem" a difficulty that happens to threaten its own views about the world. Many attempts have been made to salvage some hints of reality from this predicament. The problem is that none of these efforts assault the human-world correlate with adequate vigor. For example, some people try to save phenomenology by claiming that the human subject is not an absolute shaper of the universe, but a passive recipient of something that is "given" to it. But this supposed solution misses the point: the main problem with phenomenology was never the constituting role of the ego or its insufficient passivity over against the world. Instead, the problem is that human and world remain the only two poles of this philosophy, both of them participants in every situation of which one can possibly speak. In phenomenology, there is no relation between objects. But in our time the bar for "realism" has been set so low that fans of almost any author can claim realism on behalf of their heroes. Even the minutest trace of something coming from outside and rupturing the presence of knowledge to the human subject is flattered as a bold gesture toward the beyond. For this reason, I have concluded that the battle cry "realism," while admirable, is not enough to save us. For the weaker forms of supposed realism cannot counteract the correlationism that dominates philosophy in our time. The more important principle is to put object-object relations on exactly the same footing as subject-object relations. Only in this way can we reverse Kant's Copernican Revolution, as Whitehead already demonstrates.

By bringing inanimate objects to the fore, it might seem that we are taking the route of scientific materialism, which also rejects the precious and immaculate human subject in favor of a theory in which everything is explained by the interaction between non-human objects. But there are two problems with this materialism that lead me to reject it entirely. The first problem is that it tries to reduce the subject-object relation to the object-object relations of the brain and even smaller entities, rather than allowing for neurons to work on one level of reality and for consciousness as a whole to work on another. The second problem is that materialism's concept of object-object relations is not sufficiently realistic. For it does not raise the genuine philosophical problem of how two entities can relate, given that their reality forever withdraws into the dusk of the world. Scientific materialism performs the worthy gesture of bringing inanimate relations back into philosophy, but couples it with the dismal assertion that there is nothing beyond material impact. And here once more we encounter the great contribution of phenomenology, despite its idealism. For the greatness of Husserl is to have imported objects into the ideal realm rather than treating it in the empiricist manner as a noisy landscape of free-floating qualities. And the greatness of Heidegger is to have re-injected objects into an otherwise monolithic realm of shadowy being.

B. The Polarities in Objects

The philosophy presented in this book is not just a philosophy of objects, but of polarizations as well. Along with the real objects that exist on their own in the wilderness, there are the sensual objects discovered by Husserl that exist only in captivity: only inside the experience of some other entity. But along with objects there are also qualities, and the strange fact is that objects both have and do not have these qualities. This system of asymmetries, with two kinds of objects and two of qualities, is what led to the proposal of a fourfold structure. Those who are unwilling to accept this structure must deny one or more of the polarities it displays. And given that there are two basic axes of the fourfold, there are also two major ways of rejecting it. First, there is the usual maneuver of denying the existence of anything outside thought, as found in the Philosophy of Access rejected above. Here there is no counter-point between light and shadow, because only what is given is called real. Second, there is the empiricist claim that the object is nothing over and above its qualities, so that everything is only a bundle of directly given traits. If we put these two together as is generally done, what we end up with is a world where only one of the four poles exists: namely, *sensual qualities*. Meanwhile, scientific naturalists disdain the qualia in consciousness and try to debunk the delusions of the pathetic human mind in favor of some real substratum. And this turns out to be nothing but qualities, not a unity over and above them. In short, scientific naturalism (as is found in Brassier's position) recognizes *real qualities* as all that truly exists. But even these turn out to be only relatively different from sensual qualities, since they are entirely commensurable with some form of human access: namely, scientific knowledge. As a third option we can consider phenomenology, for which *sensual objects* are what primarily exists, since there are no real objects for Husserl outside a possible observing consciousness, and the eidetic and sensual qualities of an object are always derivative of it. That leaves us with the fourth option of a philosophy that accepts *real objects* as the only primary reality. This is the position endorsed by most classical realisms, for which unified substances are the root of everything else.

Now, after the earliest pre-Socratic philosophers considered various physical elements as the possible root constituents of the universe, Empedocles united these elements into a system in which air, earth, fire, and water were all on equal footing, mixed by love and hate. Returning to the playing card terminology utilized earlier, this book offers an analogous system to that of Empedocles: one in which spades, hearts, clubs, and diamonds are mixed by fission and fusion. The obvious difference is that the four terms of the quadruple object are not physical elements, but rather objects and qualities of every possible size, with armies and stadiums counting as "spades" (i.e. real objects) no less than droplets of water would. Instead of embracing the reductive positions of the correlationist, the naturalist, the phenomenologist, or the classical realist, object-oriented philosophy gathers the grains of truth found in all four.

C. Expanding the Theory

One of the obvious virtues of this philosophy of the fourfold object is its relative democratization of the various forms of knowledge. Hardcore reductionists easily scoff at such "soft" disciplines as sociology, art history, and music theory, assuming that these are mere human epiphenomena grafted onto a bulky stratum of real physical being. But if philosophy speaks of objects, and of their qualities and relations, then what holds true for neutrons will also hold true for governments and football teams: all of these things will be objects, and all will retain a certain identity even as their relations with various other things shift from one moment to the next. A neutron exceeds its current effects on the environment, but so does the Mubarak government in Egypt. Now, the complaint might be heard that a neutron is more real than Popeye or unicorns. And here I would agree. But the real question is whether our *concept* of a neutron is more real than our *concepts* of Popeye and unicorns, and the answer here is obviously in the negative: all three of these are sensual objects, not real ones. But it is important to note that we are not just equating a physical realm with a human one. It is not just that armies, governments, and songs have a certain reality independent of the tinier strata from which they emerge. It is also the case that there are levels *within* the physical realm. Our goal is not just to say that the humanities are irreducible to physics, but that geology and chemistry are irreducible to physics as well. Each domain has its realities, which are not reducible to where they came from. Object-oriented philosophy does not reduce, and hence offers no finger-wagging lectures to the humanities on behalf of science. Nor does it offer such lectures to science on behalf of postmodernist theories of a science constituted by the discursive practice of power.

When Freud established his principle that a dream is the symbolic fulfillment of a wish, he offered an intriguing theory of dreams. But he went much further than this. Freud's general model of desires blocked by obstacles and translated into indirect satisfaction also opened the way to theories of all human reality: slips of the tongue, forgetting objects at the home of a friend, obsessional neurosis, hysteria, psychosis, cultural realities, the death-drive, sexual difference, and even the psyches of children and animals. Regardless of how one views Freud, there is no denying the vast *scope* of psychoanalysis. In certain respects the theory of the quadruple object is even more ambitious. Like a paper lantern, the fourfold model sheds a milky and flickering light not just on the human sphere, but on inanimate causation as well. Everything both inside and outside the mind is an object that both has and does not have qualities. For this reason the theme of polarized relations between objects and qualities, split by fission and united by fusion, claims the universal subject matter that philosophy demands without arbitrarily reducing some zones of the world to others. If the quadruple object mapped in these pages is a justified model, then the four tensions, three radiations, and three junctions of ontography give us a powerful map of the cosmos from which further conclusions can easily be drawn.

Notes

1 Emmanuel Levinas, *Existence and Existents*. Translated by A. Lingis. (The Hague: Martinus Nijhoff, 1988.)

2 Jean-Luc Nancy, "Corpus." Translated by C. Sartiliot. In Nancy, *The Birth to Presence*. Translated by B. Holmes & Others. (Stanford, CA: Stanford Univ. Press, 1993.)

3 Giordano Bruno. *Cause, Principle, and Unity*. Translated by R. de Lucca. (Cambridge, UK: Cambridge Univ. Press, 1988.)

4 Gilbert Simondon, *L'individuation à la lumière des notions de forme et d'information*. (Grenoble: Millon, 2005.)

5 Manuel DeLanda. *Intensive Science and Virtual Philosophy*. (London: Continuum, 2002.)

6 Edmund Husserl, *Logical Investigations* [2 Vols.]. Translated by J. N. Findlay. (London: Routledge & Kegan Paul, 1970.)

7 Quentin Meillassoux, *After Finitude*. Translated by R. Brassier. (London: Continuum, 2008.)

8 Gilles Deleuze, *The Fold*. Translated by T. Conley. (Minneapolis: Univ. of Minnesota Press, 1993.) See for instance the following remark on page 61: "The Stoics and Leibniz invent a mannerism that is opposed to the essentialism first of Aristotle and then of Descartes."

9 Edmund Husserl, *Ideas Pertaining to a Pure Phenomenology and to a Phenomenological Philosophy (Book 1)*. Translated by F. Kersten. (Dordrecht: Springer, 1983.)

10 Kasimir Twardowski, *On the Content and Object of Presentations*. Translated by R. Grossmann. (The Hague: Martinus Nijhoff, 1977.)

11 Edmund Husserl, "Intentional Objects." In Husserl, *Early Writings in the Philosophy of Logic and Mathematics*. Translated by D. Willard. (Dordrecht: Kluwer, 1993.)

12 Maurice Merleau-Ponty, *Phenomenology of Perception*. Translated by C. Smith. (London: Routledge, 2002.)

13   Martin Heidegger, *Being and Time*. Translated by J. Macquarrie & E. Robinson. (New York: Harper & Row, 1962.)

14   Martin Heidegger, *Towards the Definition of Philosophy*. Translated by T. Sadler. (London: Continuum, 2008.)

15   Ibid., pp. 57-59.

16   Martin Heidegger, *Being and Time*, page 97. Translated by J. Macquarrie and E. Robinson. (New York: Harper and Row, 1962.)

17   Ibid., p. 99.

18   Ibid., p. 97.

19   Ibid., pp. 100-1.

20   Mark Okrent, *Heidegger's Pragmatism: Understanding, Being, and the Critique of Metaphysics*. (Ithaca, NY: Cornell University Press, 1988.)

21   Ibid., p. 31.

22   Ibid., p. 24.

23   Ibid., pp. 280-281.

24   Alfred North Whitehead, *Process and Reality*. (New York: Free Press, 1978.)

25   G.W. Leibniz, "Monadology." In *Philosophical Essays*. Translated by R. Ariew & D. Garber. (Indianapolis: Hackett, 1989.)

26   Martin Heidegger, *The Fundamental Concepts of Metaphysics: World — Finitude — Solitude*. Translated by W. McNeill & N. Walker. (Bloomington, IN: Indiana Univ. Press, 2001.)

27   Martin Heidegger, *The Question Concerning Technology, and Other Essays*. Translated by W. Lovitt. (New York: Harper & Row, 1977.)

28   Slavoj Žižek and Glyn Daly, *Conversations with Žižek*, p. 26. (Cambridge, UK: Polity Press, 2004.) Emphasis added.

29   Ibid., p. 97.

30   George Berkeley, *A Treatise Concerning the Principles of Human Knowledge*, §4. (Indianapolis: Hackett Publishing,

1982.)

31 This argument is summarized by Meillassoux in *After Finitude*, pp. 10 ff., in his fine discussion of "ancestrality" and the "archefossil."

32 *Process and Reality*, p. 6.

33 Ibid., p. 7.

34 Ibid.

35 David Stove, *The Plato Cult and Other Philosophical Follies*. (Oxford: Blackwell, 1991.)

36 Plato, *Meno*, 80d-e.

37 Saul Kripke, *Naming and Necessity*. (Cambridge, MA: Harvard Univ. Press, 1996.)

38 Francisco Suárez, *On Efficient Causality: Metaphysical Disputations 17, 18, and 19*. Translated by A. Freddoso. (New Haven: Yale University Press, 1994.)

39 Whitehead, *Process and Reality*.

40 Martin Heidegger, "Einblick in das was ist." In *Bremer und Freiburger Vorträge*. (Frankfurt: Vittorio Klostermann, 1994.)

41 Jean-François Mattéi, *Heidegger et Hölderlin: Le Quadriparti*. (Paris: PUF, 2001.)

42 Heidegger, *Poetry, Language, Thought*. Translated by A. Hofstadter. (New York: Harper, 2001.)

43 Ibid., p. 147.

44 Ibid.

45 Ibid., pp. 147-148.

46 Ibid., p. 148.

47 Ibid., p. 177.

48 See "Die Sprache," in Heidegger, *Unterwegs zur Sprache*. (Pfullingen: Günther Neske Verlag, 1959.)

49 Martin Heidegger, "The Origin of the Work of Art." In *Off the Beaten Track*. Translated by J. Young and K. Haynes. (Cambridge, UK: Cambridge Univ. Press, 2002.)

50 Friedrich Nietzsche, *Thus Spake Zarathustra*. Translated by T. Common. (New York: Dover, 1999.)

51 Martin Heidegger, *Nietzsche* [4 vols.]. Translated by D. F. Krell. (New York: Harper, 1991.)

52 Leibniz, "Monadology."

53 Xavier Zubíri, *On Essence*. Translated by A. R. Caponigri. (Washingon: Catholic Univ. of America Press, 1980.)

54 G.W. Leibniz & Samuel Clarke, *Correspondence*. Translated by R. Ariew. (Indianapolis: Hackett, 2000.)

55 Graham Harman, *Guerrilla Metaphysics: Phenomenology and the Carpentry of Things*, p. 143. (Chicago: Open Court, 2005.)

56 See for instance Manuel DeLanda, *A New Philosophy of Society*, p. 37. (London: Continuum, 2006.)

57 Heidegger, *The Fundamental Concepts of Metaphysics: World–Finitude–Solitude*. Translated by W. McNeill and N. Walker. (Bloomington, IN: Indiana University Press, 1995.)

58 David Skrbina, *Panpsychism in the West*. (Cambridge, MA: MIT Press, 2005.)

59 M.R. James, "'Oh, Whistle, and I'll Come to You, My Lad,'" p. 57. In *Casting the Runes and Other Ghost Stories*. (Oxford: Oxford University Press, 1987.)

60 Alain Badiou, *Being and Event*. Translated by O. Feltham. (London: Continuum, 2006.)

61 The event was chaired by Alberto Toscano of Goldsmiths College, University of London. A complete transcript can be found in *Collapse*, Volume III. "Speculative Realism: Ray Brassier, Iain Hamilton Grant, Graham Harman, Quentin Meillassoux," pp. 306-449.

62 For this reason the "Object-Oriented Ontology" conference in April 2010 at Georgia Tech in Atlanta featured a different lineup of speakers: Ian Bogost, Levi Bryant, and Steven Shaviro are all associated in various ways with an object-oriented approach.

63 See the aforementioned transcript in *Collapse*, Volume III, pp. 408-449.

64 Ibid., p. 409.

65 See Iain Hamilton Grant, *Philosophies of Nature After Schelling*. (London: Continuum, 2006.)
66 See Ray Brassier, *Nihil Unbound: Enlightenment and Extinction*. (London: Palgrave, 2007.)

Contemporary culture has eliminated both the concept of the public and the figure of the intellectual. Former public spaces – both physical and cultural – are now either derelict or colonized by advertising. A cretinous anti-intellectualism presides, cheerled by expensively educated hacks in the pay of multinational corporations who reassure their bored readers that there is no need to rouse themselves from their interpassive stupor. The informal censorship internalized and propagated by the cultural workers of late capitalism generates a banal conformity that the propaganda chiefs of Stalinism could only ever have dreamt of imposing. Zer0 Books knows that another kind of discourse – intellectual without being academic, popular without being populist – is not only possible: it is already flourishing, in the regions beyond the striplit malls of so-called mass media and the neurotically bureaucratic halls of the academy. Zer0 is committed to the idea of publishing as a making public of the intellectual. It is convinced that in the unthinking, blandly consensual culture in which we live, critical and engaged theoretical reflection is more important than ever before.